Acting Edition

Thornton Wilder's Playlets: Short, Short Plays for 3-5 Persons

‖SAMUEL FRENCH‖

Copyright © 2022 The Wilder Family LLC
Introduction Copyright © 2022 by A. Tappan Wilder
All Rights Reserved

THORNTON WILDER'S PLAYLETS is fully protected under the copyright laws of the United States of America, the British Commonwealth, including Canada, and all member countries of the Berne Convention for the Protection of Literary and Artistic Works, the Universal Copyright Convention, and/or the World Trade Organization conforming to the Agreement on Trade Related Aspects of Intellectual Property Rights. All rights, including professional and amateur stage productions, recitation, lecturing, public reading, motion picture, radio broadcasting, television, online/digital production, and the rights of translation into foreign languages are strictly reserved.

ISBN 978-0-573-70974-6

www.concordtheatricals.com
www.concordtheatricals.co.uk

FOR PRODUCTION INQUIRIES

UNITED STATES AND CANADA
info@concordtheatricals.com
1-866-979-0447

UNITED KINGDOM AND EUROPE
licensing@concordtheatricals.co.uk
020-7054-7298

Each title is subject to availability from Concord Theatricals Corp., depending upon country of performance. Please be aware that *THORNTON WILDER'S PLAYLETS* may not be licensed by Concord Theatricals Corp. in your territory. Professional and amateur producers should contact the nearest Concord Theatricals Corp. office or licensing partner to verify availability.

CAUTION: Professional and amateur producers are hereby warned that *THORNTON WILDER'S PLAYLETS* is subject to a licensing fee. The purchase, renting, lending or use of this book does not constitute a license to perform this title(s), which license must be obtained from Concord Theatricals Corp. prior to any performance. Performance of this title(s) without a license is a violation of federal law and may subject the producer and/or presenter of such performances to civil penalties. Both amateurs and professionals considering a production are strongly advised to apply to the appropriate agent before starting rehearsals, advertising, or booking a theatre. A licensing fee must be paid whether the title(s) is presented for charity or gain and whether or not admission is charged. Professional/Stock licensing fees are quoted upon application to Concord Theatricals Corp.

This work is published by Samuel French, an imprint of Concord Theatricals Corp.

No one shall make any changes in this title(s) for the purpose of production. No part of this book may be reproduced, stored in a retrieval system, scanned, uploaded, or transmitted in any form, by any means, now known or yet to be invented, including mechanical, electronic, digital, photocopying, recording, videotaping, or otherwise, without the prior written permission of the publisher. No one shall share this title(s), or any part of this title(s), through any social media or file hosting websites.

For all inquiries regarding motion picture, television, online/digital and other media rights, please contact Concord Theatricals Corp.

MUSIC AND THIRD-PARTY MATERIALS USE NOTE

Licensees are solely responsible for obtaining formal written permission from copyright owners to use copyrighted music and/or other copyrighted third-party materials (e.g., artworks, logos) in the performance of this play and are strongly cautioned to do so. If no such permission is obtained by the licensee, then the licensee must use only original music and materials that the licensee owns and controls. Licensees are solely responsible and liable for clearances of all third-party copyrighted materials, including without limitation music, and shall indemnify the copyright owners of the play(s) and their licensing agent, Concord Theatricals Corp., against any costs, expenses, losses and liabilities arising from the use of such copyrighted third-party materials by licensees. For music, please contact the appropriate music licensing authority in your territory for the rights to any incidental music.

IMPORTANT BILLING AND CREDIT REQUIREMENTS

If you have obtained performance rights to this title, please refer to your licensing agreement for important billing and credit requirements.

TABLE OF CONTENTS

Introduction by A. Tappan Wilder vii

The Acolyte* (1917). 1
And the Sea Shall Give Up Its Dead (1923). 7
The Angel on the Ship (1917) 13
The Angel That Troubled the Waters (1928) 19
Brother Fire (1916). 25
Centaurs (1920) 31
Childe Roland to the Dark Tower Came (1919). 37
The Christmas Interludes I* (1916). 43
The Christmas Interludes II** (1916). 49
Fanny Otcott (1918). 55
Flamingo Red (1916) 63
The Flight Into Egypt (1928) 71
Hast Thou Considered My Servant Job? (1928) 77
Leviathan (1919) 83
The Marriage We Deplore (1917) 91
The Message and Jehanne (1917). 101
Mozart and the Gray Steward (1928). 107
Nascuntur Poetae (1918). 115
Now the Servant's Name Was Malchus (1928) .121
The Penny That Beauty Spent (1918) 127
Proserpina and the Devil (1916) 133
The Song of Maria Bentedos* (1918). 139

---

*Previously unpublished, drawn from the Thornton Wilder Archives in the Yale Collection of American Literature, Beinecke Rare Book and Manuscript Library.
**Only previously published in *Oberlin* Lit Magazine (c. 1919)

INTRODUCTION

In the teens and 1920s, Wilder wrote some forty playlets, identifying them in records as "Three Minute Plays for Three Persons." About thirty of these plays were composed between 1915 and 1920, the undergraduate years he spent at Oberlin College and Yale University. (Because of lost or incomplete records, precise numbers are impossible to establish for this period.) During the decade of the '20s, Wilder wrote one playlet in 1923 and five more in 1927-1928, all tied to his hope of having a collection of playlets published in book form.

He realized this ambition in 1928. That year, thanks to his fame gained by winning the Pulitzer Prize for *The Bridge of San Luis Rey*, Wilder was able to arrange publication in the United States and in England of a volume of sixteen playlets entitled *The Angel That Troubled the Waters and Other Plays*.

Like strata of an archeological dig, these early dramatic works reveal a stunning autobiographical record of the young playwright's wonderfully romantic imagination and of the varied sources that fed it. Among these were a home where languages, art, and great books, including, of course, the Bible, were daily fare; a gypsy-like upbringing, which meant growing up and attending schools in Madison, Wisconsin; Hong Kong, Shanghai, and Chefoo, China; and Berkeley and Ojai, California; prodigious reading in drama and the history of theater; from boyhood, as many visits to theaters as he could reach by foot or trolley; his personal struggles with religion; a deep love and study of classical music; teenage crushes on specific actors and actresses; and a fascination with the meaning of art and the mysteries of the creative act.

These playlets offer a dazzling range of characters, setting, mood, and style – all the more remarkable for their compression and economy. Wilder the young playwright was trying his hand at tragedy, comedy, farce, Commedia dell'arte and even the medieval miracle play. Open this book and you will find yourself in the company of knights, saints, sinners, the Devil himself, a drunk puppeteer, talking sea serpents and donkeys, Mary and Joseph, Ibsen, Shelley and Mozart, the great actress Fanny Otcott, and the mistress of Saint Francis before he chose celibacy. Even God makes a memorable appearance – during office hours, of course.

Presenting these playlets calls for unbridled creativity and imagination in every aspect of production, from set and costume design, to use of sound and music, to staging and characterization. Directors will discover that in many if not all of these pieces, the stage directions may be spoken by a fourth performer. (In these cases a deadpan delivery is the most effective.) Because of their variety and vitality – not to mention their miniature size – these works encourage experimentation, agility and even adaptation (mini-operas and musicals, for example). They have been performed in theatrical environments ranging from stages featuring professional actors, to television studios, to classrooms, to church chancels, to fundraising events. In fact, a Wilder playlet was once produced on the surface of San Francisco Bay by a group of scullers. This should come as no surprise; because of their compression, these short-short plays are the most portable of drama, and as a result can be produced in toto anywhere, anytime.

Wherever you choose to produce these playlets, I hope you find artistic satisfaction and pleasure in experiencing the young Thornton Wilder at play.

Directors and actors seeking additional background information about Wilder's playlets may consult three widely available sources: *The Selected Letters of Thornton Wilder* (edited by Robin G. Wilder and Jackson R. Bryer, Harper, 2005); the definitive biography, *Thornton Wilder: A Life* by Penelope Niven (Harper, 2012); *The Collected Short Plays of Thornton Wilder, Volume II* (edited by Tappan Wilder, TCG Press, 1998); and *Thornton Wilder: Collected Plays & Writings on the Theatre* (edited by J.D. McClatchy, the Library of America, 2007). The last two volumes sited include Wilder's 1928 Foreword to *The Angel That Troubled the Waters and Other Plays*. Additional information is available online at www.thorntonwilder.com.

– Tappan Wilder, *July 2022*

The Acolyte

CHARACTERS
DOÑA ANNA
YZABELLE
JERONIMUS

(The scene is laid in the vestry of the old San Jeronimus in Southern California. At the back is a row of chests in which the altar cloths and vestments of the mission are kept. At the rise of the curtain, the young curator is seen ushering in two ladies. The first lady is **DOÑA ANNA SILVA DE CASTILLAS-NUEVAS**, *one of the last members of a great Spanish-Californian family. She is stout and florid and sharp, but there is yet about her an aristocratic distinction and an intellectual force. She is followed by her daughter* **YZABELLE**, *a beautiful, dark girl of nineteen with a faint suggestion of the old Spanish in her clothes. She is silent, but her eyes move about with a repressed intensity. Young* **JERONIMUS**, *who precedes them into the room, is a fair-haired boy of nineteen dressed in a black cassock tied at the waist with a black girdle. His beautiful, noble head rises from the black cassock as Galahad's arose from his armor.* **JERONIMUS'** *voice and features are sensitive and thoughtful, but he has a normal boyish smile and a large stride.)*

DOÑA ANNA. So this is where you keep the old church embroideries. It is a pity the mission has to sell them.

JERONIMUS. *(Bringing some crimson robes out of the chests.)* The Fathers have asked me to wait upon you. They could not bear to sell them themselves.

DOÑA ANNA. *(Softly.)* Look, Yzabelle, are they not beautiful? They were made by the first Indian women converts. They are copies of the originals brought by Juipero Serra from Spain, are they not?

JERONIMUS. ...Yes, Madam.

DOÑA ANNA. If your mission needs the money, there is no reason why I should feel irreligious in buying them. My daughter *(Indicating* **YZABELLE.***)* is to be married to Mr. Clevedon – Mr. Herbert Clevedon of the New York family – and we felt that it would be appropriate for her to wear for his friends some of the old embroideries of her country.

JERONIMUS. These vestments have never been worn. The Fathers were saving them until the High Mass the Holy Church will celebrate at the conversion of the whole world. They thought these Indians in California were about the last pagans in the world. But they have been hearing of the great idolatry in China and the spreading heresy that began in Germany.

DOÑA ANNA. Are they discouraged, then?

JERONIMUS. *(Simply, turning back to the chests.)* They trust in God.

DOÑA ANNA. *(Making time as she thinks of something else.)* Look, Yzabelle, we have found what we want, indeed. *(To* **JERONIMUS.***)* Does it grieve you to see these sold?

JERONIMUS. *(After a pause.)* The money is to buy a new roof for the Fathers' rooms. I think that is better. The Fathers are old and it is not good for the rain to drip into their beds.

DOÑA ANNA. Are you not old enough to be a Brother yourself?

JERONIMUS. Yes, I should be a Brother. I shall not wait much longer.

DOÑA ANNA. *(With a subtle insistence.)* I heard the Father call you Jeronimus; you have the same name as the Mission?

JERONIMUS. *(Simply.)* Yes, I was found early one morning on the altar when I was a baby. My father and mother left me there in their trouble. The Fathers named me Jeronimus, and brought me up among them. I should take the orders, for *them*, but I always ask to wait a little longer. Something inside calls to me all the time, saying to wait a little while, and I shall see the father and mother who left me on the altar in their trouble – and perhaps I have brothers and sisters too. Soon I shall give up waiting for them, though. It is my – particular – sin.

(He turns away abruptly and returns to the chest for more vestments.)

DOÑA ANNA. What is your greatest wish, Jeronimus?

JERONIMUS. *(Quietly, without hesitation.)* To kiss the hands of my mother and to see Christ in a vision.

DOÑA ANNA. *(Softly and urgently.)* These things will come to you, perhaps; but there is one thing I can do for you. I can send you to Saint Xavier's College at Monte Rosa. It was a sign that you were found on the altar; perhaps you might become a Cardinal. Will you go?

JERONIMUS. *(Pause.)* No.

DOÑA ANNA. It is a holy college; it is a school of the Church… why will you not go?

JERONIMUS. I cannot go.

DOÑA ANNA. Why not?

JERONIMUS. *(Looks at his hands on the table.)* When you asked me if I would go I listened, and in my heart I did not hear God say yes.

DOÑA ANNA. *(Marveling.)* Your life is simple for you.

JERONIMUS. When I have broken my particular sin I shall become a Brother and then all my life will be in the life of God.

(*Marveling greatly,* **DOÑA ANNA** *turns to the table covered with vestments. For a few moments, the women rest their hands on the colored cloths.*)

DOÑA ANNA. *(After a pause.)* This would look well on green.

YZABELLE. *(Rising in an unanswerable tone, in Spanish.)* Do not give any more care to the trousseau; it is unnecessary.

DOÑA ANNA. *(Impotently.)* But Yzabelle! –

YZABELLE. *(Standing.)* When you have finished you will find me in the church, waiting –

(*She goes out.*)

DOÑA ANNA. Your story has made her weep.

JERONIMUS. No; it was the sunlight on this cape that is so beautiful.

End of Play

And the Sea Shall Give Up Its Dead

CHARACTERS

A WOMAN
A STOUT LITTLE MAN
A TALL THIN DREAMY MAN

SETTING

Atlantic Abyss

(The clangor of Judgment Day's last trumpet dies away in the remotest pockets of space, and time comes to an end like a frayed ribbon. In the nave of creation, the diaphanous amphitheatre is already building for the trial of all flesh. Several miles below the surface of the North Atlantic, the spirits of the drowned rise through the water like bubbles in a neglected wineglass.)

A WOMAN. *(To the gray weeds of whose soul still cling the vestiges of color, some stained purples and some wasted reds.)* At last I could struggle no longer. My head and lungs were under intense discomfort by reason of the water with which they were filled. I said to myself: "Only think, Gertruda, you have actually arrived at the moment of death!" even then I was unwilling to believe it, though my lungs were on the point of bursting. One is never really able to believe that one will die. It is especially difficult for sovereigns who seldom, if ever, confront inevitable situations. Perhaps you know that I am Gertruda XXII, Empress of Newfoundland from 2638 to 2698?

A STOUT LITTLE MAN. Your Imperial Highness's experience is much like mine. I lived about five hundred years before Your Imperial Highness. I had always dreaded the moment of extinction, yet mine was less painful than a headache.

THE EMPRESS. We know now that the real pain comes to us in the ages that have passed since then. Have you too been swinging in mid-ocean, tangled in a cocoon of seaweed, slowly liberating your mind from the prides and prejudices and trivialities of a lifetime? That is what is painful.

A STOUT LITTLE MAN. I was a Jew and very proud of my race. Living under what I took to be the aspersions of my neighbors I had nourished the arrogant delusion that I was notable. It has taken me five hundred years of painful refection to disembarrass myself of this notion. I was a theatrical producer, and thought myself important to my time – wise, witty and kindly. Each of these ideas I have shed with a hundred times the pain of losing a limb. Now I am reconciled to the fact that I am naked, a fool, a child.

THE EMPRESS. In my life I believed fiercely that everything of which I said MY had some peculiar excellence. It was impossible to imagine a citizen proud of any country save Newfoundland, or a woman vain of any hair save the golden. I had a passion for genealogies and antiquities, and felt that such things merely looked forward to myself. Now these many years I have been wrapped in barnacles, divorcing my soul from all that it once loved. Even my love for my son and my son's love for me have vanished through sheer inconsequence. All this is the second death, and the one to be dreaded. I was afraid that when I had shed away my royalty and my beauty and my administrative talent and my pure descent and my astonishing memory for names – I was afraid that there would be nothing left. But, fortunately, underneath all this litter I have found a tiny morsel of… but dare we say the Name? – But what was yours?

A STOUT LITTLE MAN. Horatio Nissem.

THE EMPRESS. Speak to that man who is rising through the water beside you.

HORATIO NISSEM. Who are you, and what particular follies have you laid aside?

A TALL THIN DREAMY MAN. I was a priest of the gospel and a terrible time I have had taking leave of my sins. I tremble to think how but a few moments ago I still retained a longing for stupidities. Yes, sir, for the planets. I felt sure that they had personalities, and I looked forward after my death to hearing their songs. Now I know that sun and moon and stars have fallen like dust into the lap of their maker. I told myself, also, that after death I should sit through eternity overhearing the conversation of Coleridge and Augustine and Our Lord – there I should embrace my loved ones and my enemies; there I should hear vindicated before the devils the great doctrines of Infant Baptism and Sacramental Confession. Only now have I been delivered from these follies. As I swayed in the meteoric slime I begged God to punish me for certain sins of my youth, moments I well remembered of rage and pride and shame. But these seemed of no importance to him: he seemed rather to be erasing from my mind the notion that my sins were of any consequence. I see now that even the idea that I was capable of sinning was a self-flattery and an impertinence. My name was Father Cosroe: now my name is Worm.

THE EMPRESS. We still cling obstinately to our identity, as though there were something valuable in it. This very moment I feel relics of pleasure in the fact that I am myself and no one else. Yet in a moment, if there is a moment, we shall all be reduced to our quintessential matter, and you, Mr. Nissem, will be exactly indistinguishable from me. God Himself will not be able to tell the Empress of Newfoundland from the Reverend Doctor Cosroe.

HORATIO NISSEM. *(In mounting terror.)* I am afraid. I refuse to give myself up.

THE EMPRESS. Do not cry out, fool. You have awakened all my rebellious nature. O God, do not take away my identity! I do not ask for my title or my features; do not take away my myself!

HORATIO NISSEM. Do you hear? I refuse to give myself up. O God, let me not be mistaken for a Gentile.

FATHER COSROE. Your screaming has aroused my madness. Let me keep my particular mind, O God, my own curious mind, with all I have put into it!

> *(The three panic-stricken souls reach the surface of the sea. The extensive business of Doomsday is over in a twinkling, and the souls divested of all identification have tumbled, like falling stars, into the blaze of unicity. Soon nothing exists in space but the great, unwinking eye, meditating a new creation.)*

End of Play

The Angel on the Ship

CHARACTERS

VAN – the under-cook
MINNA – the captain's wife
SAM – a crew member

SETTING

The foredeck of the *Nancy Bray*, lying disabled in mid-ocean

(The figurehead of the Nancy Bray *has been torn from its place and nailed to the forepost, facing the stern – back to back, as it were, with its former position. It is the half-length of an angel bearing wreaths; she is highly colored and buxom, and has flowing yellow hair. On the deck lie three persons in the last stages of rags and exhaustion:* **MINNA**, *the remnant of a stout, coarse woman;* **VAN**, *a little, sharp youth; and a fat, old, sleepy* **JAMAICA SAM**.*)*

VAN. *(Driving the last nail into the figurehead.)* There she is. She's the new Gawd of the Atlantic. It's only a she – Gawd, but that's a good enough Gawd for a sailor.

MINNA. *(Seated on the deck.)* Us'll call her Lily. That's a name like a god's.

SAM. Youm be quick. Youm say your prayers quick.

MINNA. *(Blubbering.)* Her can't hear us. Her's just the old figgerhead we had thirty years.

VAN. Her's an angel. Her knows everything.

> *(He throws himself on his knees and lays his forehead on the boards. In a hoarse whisper:)*

That's the joss way. We all got t'do it.

> *(The others do likewise.)*

SAM. Us'll pray in turns. Us must be quick. There ain't no more water to drink, and there ain't no more sails left to carry us on. Us'll have to be quick. Youm begin, Van. Youms a great lad with the words.

VAN. *(With real fanaticism.)* Great Gawd Lily, on the ship *Nancy Bray*, all's lost with us if you don't bring us rain to drink. All the secret water I saved aside is drunk up, and we got to go over the side with the rest if you don't bring us rain today – or tomorrow. Youm allus been the angel on the front of this yere ship *Nancy Bray*, and you ain't goin' to leave us rot now. I finished my prayer, great Gawd Lily. Amen.

MINNA. Great God Lily, I'm the captain's wife that's sailed behind you for twenty years. Many's the time, great God Lily, that I shined your face so you'd look spick and span and we sailing into London in the morning, or into heathen lands. You knows everything, and you knows what I did to my husband and that I didn't let him have none of the secret water that me and Van saved up, and that when he died he knew it and cursed me and Van to hell. But youms forgiven everything and send us some rain or by-and-by we'll die and there'll be no one here prayin' to you. This is the end of my prayin', great God Lily.

VAN. *(Whispers.)* Say Amen.

MINNA. Amen, great God Lily.

SAM. I ain't goin' to pray. I'm just a dog that's been on the sea since I was born. I don' know no land eddication.

MINNA. We all got to pray for some rain.

VAN. You got t'say your word, too.

SAM. God forgive me, great God Lily, I'm old Jamaica Sam that don't never go ashore. Amen. I'd be drowned, too, only for Van and the captain's wife, who gave me some of the secret water, so that if they died I could roll 'em over the side and not leave 'em on the clean deck. Amen. Youms known my whole life, great God Lily, and how I stole the *Portagee*'s red bag, only it was almost empty, and...and that other thing. Send a lot of rain and a ship to save us. Amen.

VAN. *(Crawling up beneath the figure and throwing himself full length; hysterically.)* You've gone and forgiven me everything. Sure you have. I didn't kill the captain. The secret water was mine. Save us now, great Gawd Lily, and bring me back to my uncle in Amsterdam and make him leave me his three coal barges.

MINNA. *(Rocking herself.)* We'm lost. She'll save Sam, but I've done what the gods don't like. They'm after me. They've got me now.

(Suddenly staring off the deck.) Van! Van! Them's a ship coming to us. Van, look!

(She falls back crying.)

VAN. Them's comin'!

SAM. *(Trying to jump up and down.)* It's the *Maria Theresa Third*, comin' right at us.

VAN. *(His eye falls on the angel.)* What'll they say to the figgerhead here?

SAM. *(Sententiously.)* But that's the great God Lily. Her's saved us. You ain't goin' to do anything to her?

VAN. *(Starting to beat the angel forward with his hammer.)* They'll call us heathen, bowin' down to wood and stone. Get the rope, Sam. We'll put her back.

MINNA. *(Frightened.)* But I can't never forget her and her great starey eyes. Her I've prayed to.

End of Play

The Angel That Troubled the Waters

CHARACTERS

THE NEWCOMER – an invalid
THE MISTAKEN INVALID
THE ANGEL

SETTING

A great pool of water

(The pool: a vast, gray hall with a hole in the ceiling open to the sky. Broad stone steps lead up from the water on its four sides. The water is continuously restless and throws blue reflections upon the walls. The sick, the blind, and the malformed are lying on the steps. The long stretches of silence and despair are broken from time to time when one or another groans and turns in his rags, or raises a fretful wail or a sudden cry of exasperation at long-continued pain. A door leads out upon the porch where the attendants of the sick are playing at dice, waiting for the call to fling their masters into the water when the angel of healing stirs the pool. Beyond the porch there is a glimpse of the fierce sunlight and the empty streets of an oriental noonday.)

(Suddenly, **THE ANGEL** *appears upon the top step. His face and robe shine with a color that is both silver and gold, and the wings of blue and green, tipped with rose, shimmer in the tremulous light. He walks slowly down among the shapeless sleepers and stands gazing into the water that already trembles in anticipation of its virtue.)*

(A new invalid enters.)

THE NEWCOMER. Come, long-expected love. Come, long expected love. Let the sacred finger and the sacred breath stir up the pool. Here on the lowest step I wait with festering limbs, with my heart in pain. Free me, long-expected love, from this old burden. Since

I cannot stay, since I must return into the city, come now, renewal, come, release.

> *(Another invalid wakes suddenly out of a nightmare, calling: "The Angel! The Angel has come. I am cured." He flings himself into the pool, splashing his companions. They come to life and gaze eagerly at the water. They hang over the brink, and several slide in. Then a great cry of derision rises: "The fool! Fool! His nightmare again. Beat him! Drive him out into the porch."* **THE MISTAKEN INVALID** *and his dupes drag themselves out of the water and lie dripping disconsolately upon the steps.)*

THE MISTAKEN INVALID. I dreamt that an angel stood by me and that at last I should be free of this hateful place and its company. Better a mistake and this jeering than an opportunity lost.

> *(He sees* **THE NEWCOMER** *beside him and turns on him plaintively.)*

Aïe! you have no right to be here, at all events. You are able to walk about. You pass your days in the city. You come here only at great intervals, and it may be that by some unlucky chance you might be the first one to see the sign. You would rush into the water and a cure would be wasted. You are yourself a physician. You have restored my own children. Go back to your work and leave these miracles to us who need them.

THE NEWCOMER. *(Ignoring him; under his breath.)* My work grows faint. Heal me, long-expected love; heal me that I may continue. Renewal, release; let me begin again without this fault that bears me down.

THE MISTAKEN INVALID. I shall sit here without ever lifting my eyes from the surface of the pool. I shall be the next. Many times, even since I have been here, many times the angel has passed and has stirred the water, and hundreds have left the hall leaping and crying out with joy. I shall be the next.

> (**THE ANGEL** *kneels down on the lowest step and meditatively holds his finger poised above the shuddering water.*)

THE ANGEL. Joy and fulfillment, completion, content, rest and release have been promised.

THE NEWCOMER. Come, long-expected love.

THE ANGEL. *(Without turning makes himself apparent to* **THE NEWCOMER** *and addresses him.)* Draw back, physician, this moment is not for you.

THE NEWCOMER. Angelic visitor, I pray thee, listen to my prayer.

THE ANGEL. Healing is not for you.

THE NEWCOMER. Surely, surely, the angels are wise. Surely, O prince, you are not deceived by my apparent wholeness. Your eyes can see the nets in which my wings are caught; the sin into which all my endeavors sink half-performed cannot be concealed from you.

THE ANGEL. I know.

THE NEWCOMER. It is no shame to boast to an angel of what I might yet do in love's service were I but freed from this bondage.

THE MISTAKEN INVALID. Surely the water is stirring strangely today! Surely I shall be whole!

THE ANGEL. I must make haste. Already the sky is afire with the gathering host, for it is the hour of the new song among us. The earth itself feels the preparation in the skies and attempts its hymns. Children born in this hour spend all their lives in a sharper longing for the perfection that awaits them.

THE NEWCOMER. Oh, in such an hour was I born, and doubly fearful to me is the flaw in my heart. Must I drag my shame, prince and singer, all my days more bowed than my neighbor?

THE ANGEL. *(Stands a moment in silence.)* Without your wound where would your power be? It is your very remorse that makes your low voice tremble into the hearts of men. The very angels themselves cannot persuade the wretched and blundering children on earth as can one human being broken on the wheels of living. In love's service only the wounded soldiers can serve. Draw back.

> *(He swiftly kneels and draws his finger through the water. The pool is presently astir with running ripples. They increase, and a divine wind strikes the gay surface. The waves are flung upon the steps.* **THE MISTAKEN INVALID** *casts himself into the pool, and the whole company lurches, rolls, or hobbles in. The servants rush in from the porch. Turmoil. Finally, the no-longer* **MISTAKEN INVALID** *emerges and leaps joyfully up the steps. The rest, coughing and sighing, follow him.* **THE ANGEL** *smiles for a moment and disappears.)*

THE HEALED MAN. Look, my hand is new as a child's. Glory be to God! I have begun again.

(To **THE NEWCOMER.***)* May you be the next, my brother. But come with me first, an hour only, to my home. My son is lost in dark thoughts. I – I do not understand him, and only you have ever lifted his mood. Only an hour…my daughter, since her child has died, sits in the shadow. She will not listen to us…

End of Play

Brother Fire

CHARACTERS

ANNUNZIATA – a peasant woman
ISOLA – her daughter, about eight
BROTHER FRANCIS – their friend

SETTING

A hut in the mountains of northern Italy

(**ANNUNZIATA** *is preparing the evening meal over the fire.* **ISOLA** *is playing beside her.*)

ANNUNZIATA. Now, now! Not so near. One of these days you'll be falling into the fire, and there'll be nothing left to tell us about you but your shoes. Put them on and get out the bowls for supper.

ISOLA. I like to play with the fire.

ANNUNZIATA. What a thing to say!

ISOLA. I'd like to let my hair into it, gently, gently, gently, gently.

ANNUNZIATA. Don't you hear me tell you it's a wicked thing?

ISOLA. Brother Francis says it's our brother, and one of the best things in the world.

ANNUNZIATA. Tchk, tchk! – What makes the starling sing in his cage all of a sudden?

ISOLA. It's Brother Francis himself looking at us.

ANNUNZIATA. Tell him to come in and have some supper.

ISOLA. Come in, my mother says, and have some supper.

(**BROTHER FRANCIS** *appears at the door. He blesses the house.*)

BROTHER FRANCIS. I can very well go on to my own supper and need not lighten your kettle.

ANNUNZIATA. Come in, Brother Francis. What you take will not even make a new ring around the kettle. Besides, I see you have been up to the top of the mountain again. You are cold and wet. Come and sit by the fire.

BROTHER FRANCIS. Yes, I have been up to the very top since yesterday, among the rocks and the birds in the rocks. Brother Wind was there and Sister Rain was there, but Brother Fire was not.

ANNUNZIATA. Now you sit by him, Isola, while I get some more wood; but don't ask him any questions. Now, Brother, put this fur skin across your knees.

(She goes out.)

ISOLA. What did you do, Brother Francis?

BROTHER FRANCIS. I watched and waited to see what they would let me see. For a long while there was nothing; then they nodded to one another, meaning that it was permitted to me. I watched seven stars closely. Suddenly they turned and fed inwards, and I saw the Queen of Heaven leading forth her company before all the shipwrecked seamen of this world. – However, do not tell thy mother, for she believes in no one's miracles but her own.

ISOLA. My mother says the fire is a wicked thing.

BROTHER FRANCIS. *(Turning.)* What, Sister Annunziata, how can you say that? – Why, what would cook your broth, what would keep you warm? And when you return from the mountaintops, what else shines out from all the friendly windows of the world? Look at its flames, how they lean towards us!

ISOLA. It says: Give me something to eat. Give me something to eat.

BROTHER FRANCIS. *(Excitedly.)* Yes, yes. Its warmth is a kind of hunger. I have a love for all things in fur, feathers and scales, but I have not less a love for the fire that warms us.

(He edges the cloak into the fire.)

Look how it reaches for it. Wicked? Wicked? Never.

ISOLA. But, Brother Francis, it will…it will…

(The flames suddenly seize the cloak. **BROTHER FRANCIS** *rises, wrapped in fire.)*

Brother Francis, you are on fire! Mother, Mother!

(She rushes from the hut and returns with her mother. **ANNUNZIATA** *snatches the fur from* **BROTHER FRANCIS** *and throws it into the hearth.)*

BROTHER FRANCIS. *(Still standing ecstatically with lifted hands.)* Eat, Brother Fire. I knew you wanted this. I knew that you loved me too.

(He looks about him; then ruefully to **ANNUNZIATA***:)*

Sister, you have spoiled his supper.

ANNUNZIATA. *(With somber and averted face.)* I do not know what you mean. Here is your bowl of broth. Sit down and eat it.

BROTHER FRANCIS. Sister, do not be angry with me.

ANNUNZIATA. *(Breaking out.)* Come now, should we kill everything, the animals for their furs, yes, and one another, to feed them to the fire? Is it not enough that it takes our good pine tree by our road? There, that is logic, Brother Francis.

BROTHER FRANCIS. Bring me not logic, Sister. She is the least of the handmaids of love. I am often troubled when she speaks.

ANNUNZIATA. Must we give what makes us often warm for that which makes us warm only for a moment?

BROTHER FRANCIS. *(Waving his wooden spoon about humorously.)* My mind is strangely light tonight, like the flames that play about the relics of Saint James. I could wander again through the whole night.

ANNUNZIATA. Where is your mother that she should watch over you? Had I not these other duties I should leave everything and watch over you myself.

BROTHER FRANCIS. She is in Paradise with a golden crook, leading the fames that died of hunger in this wicked world. She leads them to pasture on drifts of dried leaves. Look, Isola, I know that there is fame to burn all evil in the Lake of the Damned. I do not speak of that now, but I know also that fire is at all times useful to the great Blessed. It surrounds them and they dwell in it.

And even now...

(And so on.)

End of Play

Centaurs

CHARACTERS

SHELLEY – the poet
HILDA WANGEL – a character in Ibsen
IBSEN – the playwright

SETTING

A theatre

(The usual chattering audience of our theatres is waiting for the curtains to part on a performance of Ibsen's The Master Builder. *Presently the lights are lowered to a colored darkness, and the warm glow of the footlights begins again the ancient magic. The orchestra draws its bows soothingly to a gradual close and files out gropingly into the rabbit hutch prepared for it, leaving perhaps a sentimental viola player staring upward into the darkness. Suddenly, the curtains are parted by an earnest young man, who stares into the shadowy audience and starts, with some difficulty, to address it.)*

SHELLEY. My name is Shelley. I... I am told that some of you may have heard of me, may even know my poems – or some of my poems. I cannot imagine what they may seem like to you who live in this world that...that is, I have just seen your streets for the first time – your machines, your buildings, and especially the machines with which you talk to one another. My poems must seem very strange in a world of such things.

(Awkward pause.)

Well, I wanted to say something about this play, but I don't know how to put it into words for you. You see, I feel that, in part, I wrote this play.

(With sudden relief, calling back through the curtains:)

Hilda! Will you help me a moment?

HILDA WANGEL. *(Offstage.)* Yes, I'm coming.

SHELLEY. *(Constrainedly, to the audience.)* A friend of mine.

(**HILDA** *appears in her mountaineering costume of the first act, carrying an alpenstock.*)

HILDA. *(Vigorously, to the audience.)* He promised to do this by himself, but he has gotten into difficulties. Have you told them that you wrote it?

SHELLEY. I tried to. It didn't sound reasonable.

HILDA. Well, you were able to explain it to me. Help me to persuade Papa to come out here.

(She disappears.)

SHELLEY. Henrik, for my sake.

HILDA. *(Offstage.)* There, did you hear that? For his sake, he said. Miss Fosli, will you kindly push forward the wicker settee from the last act? Thank you.

(A wicker settee suddenly appears.)

Now, Papa.

(**HILDA** *reappears leading the dramatist.* **IBSEN** *is smiling sternly through his spectacles and through his fringe of upcurling white whiskers.*)

Now sit down and Shelley will begin again.

IBSEN. Hurry, young man. My beautiful play is ready to begin. The kingdom is on the table, the nurseries are empty, and this house is full of unconverted people.

HILDA. *(Touching his shoe with the tip of her alpenstock.)* Hush, Papa. Let him go about it in his own way. Have you told them about the poem you were about to write when you died?

SHELLEY. No. *(To the audience.)* Ladies and Gentlemen, on the day I died – drowned in the Mediterranean – I was full of a poem to be called "The Death of a Centaur," that I did not have time to put on paper.

HILDA. You forgot to say that it was a very good poem.

SHELLEY. I couldn't say that.

HILDA. You said it to me. *(Turning to the audience.)* You should know that this young man had come to a time when everything he wrote was valuable. He was as sure to write great poems as a good apple tree is to give good apples.

SHELLEY. Perhaps it would have been one of the better ones. At all events, it was never written...

IBSEN. *(Rising excitedly and stamping his feet as though they had snow on them.)* And I claim that I wrote it. The poem hung for a while above the Mediterranean, and then drifted up toward the Tyrol, and I caught it and wrote it down. And it is *The Master Builder*.

HILDA. Now you must sit down, Papa, and keep calm. We must reason this out calmly. In the first place, both are certainly about centaurs. What do you say, Shelley?

SHELLEY. Well, it is not a strange idea, or a new one, that the stuff of which masterpieces are made drifts about the world waiting to be clothed with words. It is a truth that Plato would have understood that the mere language, the words of a masterpiece, are the least of its offerings. Nay, in the world we have come into now, the languages of the planet have no value; but the impulse, the idea of "Comus" is a miracle, even in heaven. Let you remember this when you regret the work that has been lost through this war that has been laid upon your treasurable young men. The work they might have done is still with you, and will yet find its way into your lives and into your children's lives.

IBSEN. Enough, enough! You will be revealing all the mysteries soon. Enough has been said to prove that "The Death of a Centaur" and *The Master Builder* are the same poem. Get in with you, children. The play is ready to start. Solness sits with his head in his hands, and the harps are in the air.

> *(He goes behind the curtains.* **SHELLEY** *lingers a moment; a shadow has fallen across his face.)*

HILDA. *(Laying her hand on his arm.)* What is the matter?

SHELLEY. That reminded me…of another poem…I did not write down.

End of Play

Childe Roland to the Dark Tower Came

CHARACTERS

CHILDE ROLAND – a knight
THE GIRL
THE DARK GIRL

SETTING

Near the scene of battle

(The sun has set over the great marsh, leaving a yellow-brown Flemish light upon the scene. In the midst of the mire and among the tufts of iron-grass stands an old, round tower. Its lower narrow door is of green bronze, scarred with many assaults. Above the door are two small windows, behind which a gleam seems to come and go.)

(In the half-light that hangs over the plain, a man in armor stumbles through the bog to the single step before the door. He is many times wounded; his blood flows freely to the ground; the knight blows his horn; the landscape collects itself to listen.)

CHILDE ROLAND. I die... Open the door to me.

(The landscape laughs, then falls suddenly silent. Presently, its subterranean waters are again heard sucking at buried tree trunks.)

I have seen your lights here from a long way off...you cannot hide from me now.

*(The marsh becomes animated and fully interested in the stranger. One of the windows brightens slightly and a **GIRL** looks out. Her voice and manner are strangely detached and impersonal, as though she had been called away from some absorbing interest, and was eager to return to it.)*

Oh, you are here! Quick, descend to me. All my wounds are flowing. I am dying of thirst.

THE GIRL. Who are you to issue commands against this tower? Some emperor, surely.

CHILDE ROLAND. My name is written with many another upon the sword of Charlemagne: That is enough.

THE GIRL. You are some king, perhaps – driven into the wilderness by your not too loving subjects?

CHILDE ROLAND. No king, but a friend and soldier of kings.

THE GIRL. Oh! This is some wise counselor. If you are so wise we will quickly open the door to you.

CHILDE ROLAND. Not wise, but often listened to in grave matters, having a voice equal with many others.

THE GIRL. *(Utterly untouched, lightly to someone within.)* I do believe this is some sweet singer. Let us bind on our slippers right quickly and put red wine to his lips, for poets are ever our delight.

CHILDE ROLAND. I am no singer, but one loving the string and the voice at all times. Open the door! For the wind is cold on the marsh, and the first terrible stars are stepping into their chains. Open the door, for my veins are emptied on your sill.

THE GIRL. *(Leaning far out, while her red hair falls almost to his shoulders.)* Beat upon the door, Sir Knight. Many things are gained by force.

CHILDE ROLAND. My hands are strengthless... I am fallen on my knees... Pity me!

> *(***THE GIRL** *laughs pleasantly to her companion within.)*

Reach over the stars to me, Mary, Mother of God. To you I was committed in my first year, and have renewed yearly my promises. Send from thy golden mind and thy voiceless might the issue out of this difficulty.

*(A **SECOND GIRL**, dark and thoughtful, appears at the other window.)*

THE GIRL. *(Intimately.)* He is praying now.

THE DARK GIRL. He is a little boy. His thoughts this last hour are returning to his earliest year.

THE GIRL. Is it not beautiful that a knight should think of a little child?

THE DARK GIRL. What brought you here, Knight-at-Arms?

CHILDE ROLAND. The battle passed suddenly into the west. This tower was all I could see. And here I brought my wounds.

THE GIRL. *(Softly.)* You see he is still able to reason; he reasons very well.

THE DARK GIRL. What led you to think that we could help you?

CHILDE ROLAND. I know your name! All my life I have heard of this tower. They say that on the outside you are dark and unlovely, but that within every hero stands with his fellows and the great queens step proudly on the stair.

THE DARK GIRL. And do you believe this?

CHILDE ROLAND. *(After a pause.)* Yes. *(With sudden fury.)* Open the door! There is a place for me within. Open the door, Death!

THE GIRL. *(Drawing up her hair languidly.)* He is irresistible, this great man.

CHILDE ROLAND. Oliver! Oliver! Charlemagne! I hear your voices. It is I, Roland, without, in the dark marsh. My body I cast away for you. My breath I returned to the sky in your defense. Open the door!

(The marsh is a little put out by all this strong feeling. It lies quiet. The door slowly opens

upon a hall full of drifting, violet mists, some of which escape and fade over the marsh. **THE GIRL** *with the red hair is seen walking away in the hall, her mocking face looking back over her shoulder.* **THE DARK GIRL,** *robed in gray, leans across the threshold, extending a chalice to the knight's lips.)*

THE DARK GIRL. Take courage, high heart. How slow you have been to believe well of us. You gave us such little thought while living that we have made this little delay at your death.

End of Play

The Christmas Interludes I

CHARACTERS

LEAH
BARSHAEL
THE GIRL

*(The scene is the kitchen of the Inn in Bethlehem. On a low stool before the fire sits a small, coarse woman – **LEAH**, the cook. She is staring into the fire, her long, muscular arms encircling her knees. Presently, the door opens and admits a great dark man wrapped in a red blanket. He pushes his shepherd's crook into a corner and comes to the fire.)*

LEAH. Why are you leaving the sheep this way? You'll get into trouble if you're missed.

BARSHAEL. There are enough of them there to take care of the sheep.

LEAH. It's only by chance that the door isn't barred up for the night.

BARSHAEL. You'd have unbarred it for me if I'd knocked.

LEAH. What else could I do! – against a strong man like you. *(Going to the door.)* It's after midnight. Have you just come straight from the hill?

BARSHAEL. No, I've been waiting around the yard until that other girl got out of here. She's gone for the night, hasn't she?

LEAH. No, she's just gone into the stable to carry some grain to the cows. She forgot to do it before. She dreams around all day over what the crazy old man in his tower above the wine shop tells her.

BARSHAEL. She always looks at you with that law-and-the-Prophets kind of look. I don't like her around.

LEAH. Oh, don't mind her. She don't say a word now since I scolded her. It's funny that a fine kind of man like you – ! Oh well, we're all afraid of different things. I won't go into the stable anymore. Two people came tramping along with a donkey and we, of course, told 'em there wasn't no room here – we're expectin' great folks any minute, the master says. And so she, bein' very tired asked to take rooms in the stable. And the queerest eyes she had!

> *(The door opens and* **THE GIRL** *enters slowly. In one hand, she holds the basket for grain. She closes the door quietly, putting her back to it, and stares at the ceiling. The other two watch her expectantly.)*

THE GIRL. *(In a low, tense voice.)* There's a baby been born in the stable!

LEAH. I thought so! *(Angrily.)* I've got a good mind to drive 'em on and make 'em learn a lesson. Some women don't care –

THE GIRL. Hush – it is the child we look for. I know it is The Child we look for. The old man in the tower has seen a new star above this roof.

LEAH. *(Scornfully.)* And what does the tramp of a father say of the child? I suppose he said it's David's son, too?

THE GIRL. Yes...

LEAH. And the mother, too. I suppose that she got up and cried: "A greater than Abraham! He that shall redeem His people!"

THE GIRL. So young she is! –

LEAH. Well, let her look out that that terrible one-eyed cow doesn't trample on the expected of His People. Because then, you know, we might have to wait another thousand years.

THE GIRL. But that is how I *know*! He is lying in the manger of that very cow. But she has knelt down on the straw and did only breathe on the child and turned away. I cannot get near her, but these people walk about in her stall.

LEAH. Bolt the door now and let's not hear any more prophecy from you. Tomorrow I'll attend to these travellers.

THE GIRL. *(To* **BARSHAEL.***)* All the other shepherds that were with you have come in and are singing there. They have seen angels on the hill – and you were not there.

BARSHAEL. *(Striking her.)* Why do you say that to me, daughter of a camel-eater?

THE GIRL. I am the first that have seen my King, therefore you strike me.

End of Play

The Christmas Interludes II

CHARACTERS

ST. JOSEPH
SERVING-MAID
MARIA

(The scene being made plain showeth forth that stable in Bethlehem [whereof it is written in The Book, as scholars declare]. In the manger lies the Holy Child unseen. **OUR LADY** *sleeps beside on a bed of sweet hay.* **ST. JOSEPH** *stands beside to guard.)*

ST. JOSEPH. I am Saint Joseph. Unto me was given
To watch o'er those who are the bliss of Heaven!
Here in this manger lies Earth's slighted guest
Through whose forgiveness heathen lands are blest.
And on that straw in mantle blue
Maria lies – who prayeth God for you.
And what we play now let your hearts attend;
Lo, know your Savior, King and Friend;
But if you lead your thoughts astray
To you be lost this Christmas Day.

(Here let be played that sweet music which Charles of Benicet wrote for those who play the viol by the Church of Notre Dame de Ytelle, and can be had from the verger at the little door that looketh upon the fields.)

(Here entereth a **SERVING-MAID** *bringing grain in a vessel.)*

SERVING-MAID. I am a serving-maid that in this hostel live.
This grain to horse and ass and cow I give
When all are gathered in, and evening comes.
To-day the inn was full and all the rooms,
So in this stable certain travellers stay.

One was a girl. I cannot say
How sweet and sad she was; or with what grace
She did accept perforce this humble place.
 – But now I fear,
For hard by here
A wise man in a tower dwells
Who gazes at the sky and tells
What stars there are. And now he says
Seven stars do hang above this place
That do not move in their celestial way
With Bear and Bowman fleeing from the day.

ST. JOSEPH. *(Here doth see the* **MAID.***)* What do you here?
For two are sleeping still;
To waken them would be thy grievous ill.

SERVING-MAID. I will be swift and soft my task to do
And grain inside these mangers strew.

> *(Here she goeth to pour grain into the mangers, but starteth back with a cry.)*

All ye who stretch the wing in Paradise,
What is this light-full thing before my eyes!
O gentle child! Thy eyes are open wide;
The cows you fear not nor fear me beside.
Art thou of earth, O grave and mild?
Blessed the mother of so fair a child.

(Here waketh **OUR GOOD LADY.***)*

MARIA. Thou art the first thy "hail" to say;
A thousand following come this lowly way.
Think of this blossoming night; and of the Rose
That now from Jesse's stem in wonder grows,

Whose perfume puts to sleep all martyr folk.
Beneath the lion's mane or tyrant's stroke.
The thornless Rose that must be crowned with thorns,
That, falling earth, the firmament adorns.
That will upraise the Dead, yet walk in Hell,
And die in thirst, the Everlasting Well.

ST. JOSEPH. Here's gold; go buy us dates and bread;
Archangels speed thee; art by Prophets led.

SERVING-MAID. Love be my speed; oh kiss me, Lady that I haste,
And mention my sad Judas when thou prayest,
Six years he is, but will not let me touch
or hold him, love or sing or such,
Tho he be mine, my only – brother, family;
and hath that lack of love for me!

(Here she hasteth away.)

MARIA. I will not weep; my heart is stricken sore;
My joy, how great! My grief the more and more;
But let us sing the Christmastide aloud –
Anon we fall the tear and weave the shroud.

(Here shall be performed The Shepherd's Play *as if oft given; and shall follow, if thy Bishop permit,* The Merry Play of the Man who has Married a Dumb Wife.*)*

End of Play

---

*Note: Here Wilder references Anatole France's comedy of 1912.

Fanny Otcott

CHARACTERS

MRS. OTCOTT – an actress
SAMPSON – a servant
ATCHESON – an old friend of Mrs. Otcott's

SETTING

Outside Mrs. Otcott's home

(**MRS. OTCOTT**, *that great actress in the tradition of the Siddons, the Oldfeld, Bracegirdle, O'Neill, is spending a quiet month in Wales. We do not see the cottage, we do not even see the mountains, but there is a stretch of lawn on whose gentle slope there stands an ancient, round tower overgrown with ivy. In the shadow of this Arthurian monument,* **MRS. OTCOTT** *has placed a table whereon she is sorting old engravings, playbills, letters, contracts, ribbons; in short, her past. She is still the handsome, humorous, Irish soul from whom every item out of the old trunks exacts its exclamation, its gesture, its renewed indignation or pleasure. She is attended by a boy in livery, half-asleep against a flowerpot.)*

MRS. OTCOTT. Sampson! Tay!

SAMPSON. *(Springing up.)* Yes, ma'am. Wid or widout a streak o' cream?

MRS. OTCOTT. Widout. And Sampson, tell Pence I am not at home. Not even to the one in the yellow curls, or to the good black beard. And if they seem to know that I am at home, tell them...that I have gone up the tower, or that I have the vapors.

SAMPSON. You wants tea widout, and tell Mrs. Pence you don't want to see none of de gentlemen from de village inn – dat you has de vapors.

MRS. OTCOTT. There! Do you see that, Sampson? I wore that the night the king dined with me on the stage.

SAMPSON. *(His eyes as big as soup plates.)* King...James!

MRS. OTCOTT. *(Shuddering.)* No, stupid – Charles. – Go away! This afternoon I shall devote to another woman, to another and a different woman, and yet to myself, to myself, to myself.

SAMPSON. I'll tell Mrs. Pence.

> *(He goes out.* **MRS. OTCOTT** *picks up a packet of letters. One look, tosses them away, then rises, muttering; goes and stamps on them and laughs. She returns to pick up a playbill and reads the heading with glistening eyes: "Fanny Otcott as Faizella in* The Princess of Cathay. *First time." She strides about, lost in thought. She almost walks into a gentleman who has entered through the hedge. He is wearing a black hat and cape, and has a serious, worn face.)*

ATCHESON. Your servant, Mrs. Otcott.

MRS. OTCOTT. *(Thunderstruck.)* Why, *no*! Yes! By the garter, it is George Atcheson. Oh! Oh! Oh!

ATCHESON. I do not disturb you, Mrs. Otcott? I... I came to discuss a thing that is very serious to me.

MRS. OTCOTT. *(Suddenly very pleased.)* Everything is – sit down, my friend. You always were very serious. That's why you made such a bad Hamlet. Delay your serious talk, George, and tell me about the women you have loved since you loved me, and confess that I finally made them all unendurable to you.

ATCHESON. You misunderstand me, Mrs. Otcott...

MRS. OTCOTT. *(Loudly.)* Fanny.

ATCHESON. Ah... Fanny?

MRS. OTCOTT. All you need is a little coaxing. Well, George, a woman drove you on to the stage when you were preparing for the church, and a woman drove you off, and it was my greatest service to the stage. Look, George, you remember me as Faizella in *The Princess of Cathay*. I never did better than that. Great Rufus, you played opposite me in it. Look!

ATCHESON. Perhaps you remember... I lost consciousness...

MRS. OTCOTT. Ah yes! The pale divinity student fainted. Oh! George, you were the first of my lovers. No, it wasn't love, perhaps, but it was beautiful. It was like hawthorn buds and meadowlarks and Mr. Handel's water music. And since, I have never ceased searching for love. Perhaps love strikes the first time or never at all. Then I was too much in love with my work. And, oh, George, how young we were! But you were very dear to me in the old garret, and I'm sorry to see you're growing stout, for it's one more reminder that I shall probably live and die without having known the lightning of love.

(She sits down with a great flow of silken draperies and shakes her head at him ruefully.)

ATCHESON. I have come to discuss our...our association...

MRS. OTCOTT. Thunder and hell! Don't you call that an association!

ATCHESON. ...But my view of it is very different.

*(**MRS. OTCOTT**'s shoe commences to mark time nervously on the turf.)*

After my retirement from the stage I resumed my theological studies, and I am now Bishop of Westholmstead.

(The shoe is now motionless.)

None of my friends know of that...that experience in my life, but it has always remained as a bitter...as a distressing spot in my conscience.

MRS. OTCOTT. *(After a pause, very rapidly.)* I see, you want to make a clean breast of the perilous stuff. You want to make a public confession, probably. You are married?

ATCHESON. Yes.

MRS. OTCOTT. You have several sons probably?

ATCHESON. Yes.

MRS. OTCOTT. And you lie awake nights, saying: "Hypocrisy, hypocrisy."

(Pause.)

Well, make your confession. But why consult me?

ATCHESON. I have followed your course, madam, and seen the growing admiration your art commands in court – I might almost say in the church.

MRS. OTCOTT. You do not suppose that that revelation would cast any deeper shadow on the good name of Fanny Otcott, such as it is. Remember, George, the months you call sinful. It wasn't love, perhaps, but it was grace and poetry. The heavens rained odors on us. It was as childlike and harmless as paintings on fans. I was a girl tragedienne reciting verses endlessly before a mirror and you were a young student who for the first time had seen a young girl braid her hair and sing at her work. Since then you have learned long names of books and heard a great many sneers from women as old as myself. You have borrowed your ideas from those who have never begun to live and who dare not.

ATCHESON. *(His head in his hands and his elbows on his knees.)* I do not know what to think. Your reasoning is full of perils.

MRS. OTCOTT. Go away and tell your congregations what you please. I feel as though you were communicating to my mind some of those pitiable remorses that have weakened you. I have sinned, but I have not that year on my conscience. It is that year and my playing of Faizella that will bring troops of angels to welcome me to Paradise. Go away and tell your congregations what you please.

ATCHESON. You give me no help in the matter, Mrs. Otcott.

MRS. OTCOTT. Go away. In the name of Heaven, go!

> *(Crooked with doubt and hesitation, the Bishop of Westholmstead goes out through the hedge. For a few moments,* **MRS. OTCOTT** *sits on the table, swinging one foot and muttering savagely in an imaginary conversation. Reenter* **SAMPSON** *with a tray.)*

SAMPSON. Three gentlemen waited on you from de village inn, but Mrs. Pence sent dem away. She said you was up de tower, ma'am.

MRS. OTCOTT. *(Showily.)* Go call them back, Sampson. Tell them I have come down from de tower. Bring up the best box of wine – the one with my picture painted on it. I shall be young again.

End of Play

Flamingo Red:
A Comedy in Danger

CHARACTERS

MADAME FLAMINGO
CHARLES
DORA

*(The Flamingo Red Tea Room of the Hotel Coeur de Lion is a medievally furnished room, toned to its own color in every possible detail. The wall hangings, the carpets, the teacups, are all of the same light red; the only noticeable exceptions being the silver of the tea sets and the white of the tablecloths. The dispenser of tea, gowned in a model possible to Guinevere and in the same disturbing hue, is a mystic temperament, and we cannot do less than call her **MADAME FLAMINGO**. A door at the back opens and admits a very young man and a very young lady – as self-conscious as two little birds. **MADAME FLAMINGO** leads them to a table almost overhanging our orchestra.)*

MADAME FLAMINGO. Tea, I suppose?

THE YOUNG MAN. Chicken broth for me.

THE YOUNG LADY. Do I want chicken broth, Charles?

CHARLES. Yes, very badly. And some oyster crackers.

THE YOUNG LADY. No, I want tea.

CHARLES. You'll wish you'd asked for chicken broth.

THE YOUNG LADY. I'll halve it. I want beef tea!

(She is delighted with herself. She looks up to see if **CHARLES** *is amused.)*

CHARLES. *(To* **MADAME FLAMINGO.***)* We'll let her have beef tea.

*(**MADAME FLAMINGO** smiles maternally and goes out.)*

THE YOUNG LADY. What's this room called?

CHARLES. The Peacock Blue Bouillon Room.

THE YOUNG LADY. (*Protesting.*) Do be serious sometimes. It's the Flamingo Red Room.

CHARLES. Oh! Who'd have thought it!

DORA. I don't like it.

CHARLES. Hush. Madame Flamingo'll hear you.

DORA. I want to sit on that side of the table.

CHARLES. Weigh the matter well. If you want to sit here badly, do; but let's not keep changing.

DORA. (*Firmly.*) Yes. I want to sit there.

CHARLES. (*As they change.*) If you want to move back don't say so.

DORA. (*Sitting down.*) No, I don't like this after all. (*Firmly.*) I want to come back. I don't like this room.

CHARLES. Oh Dora, you never used to be this way. (*Changing wearily.*) Come on.

DORA. You musn't say things like that. Look at how long we've been married, and yet you criticize me the whole time.

(**MADAME FLAMINGO** *returns with their wants.*)

MADAME FLAMINGO. Beef tea. Chicken broth.

(*She hovers around the back of the room.*)

DORA. No. I want the chicken broth. You can have the beef tea. The chicken broth is so pretty.

CHARLES. I was just thinking that I wanted the beef tea instead.

DORA. (*Doubtfully.*) Were you? Then I think I'll keep the beef tea, if you don't mind at all. It's so nice and dark.

CHARLES. *(Firmly.)* You can't do this all our life, Dora.

DORA. It's perfectly simple. I'm drinking what I ordered. You're drinking what you ordered. Isn't that all right?

CHARLES. No. You mustn't be wayward that way. Decide for yourself what you're going to have and then keep to it; and leave some time to talk about things worth while.

DORA. Things worth while! And you're always making a joke of everything!

CHARLES. You know what I mean better than I do. How is your beef tea?

DORA. *(Pushing it away.)* I don't want it. You've spoiled it for me. You're always criticizing.

CHARLES. It shan't come up again. I'm sorry. They're very charming – the little ways you've got. Drink the beef tea of peace and love me again.

DORA. Oh, I love you even when I'm mad, but you are so funny sometimes –

(She lays her hand along the tablecloth.)

CHARLES. *(Hitting it playfully.)* Go away, sir, go away.

DORA. *(Flaring up.)* I told you not to do that.

CHARLES. *(Put out.)* Oh, very well.

DORA. When you know I don't like a thing, I think you might stop it.

CHARLES. I thought you were playing. You were playing at first. How am I to know when you're going to get angry or not?

DORA. When I say not to do a thing, just stop.

CHARLES. That's all very well, but – Oh, eat your beef tea, and let's get out.

DORA. *(Angry.)* What were you going to say, Charles Darth?

CHARLES. *(Ditto.)* You must learn to do a thing through and through, Dora, without fights here and there, and touchiness and everything else.

> *(She rises and picks up her gloves with an exclamation of supreme disillusion.)*
>
> *(**MADAME FLAMINGO** comes forward hurriedly.)*

MADAME FLAMINGO. Won't you please sit down a moment? I have something to tell you.

DORA. *(Calling into her seat.)* What is it?

MADAME FLAMINGO. This room as you know is the Flamingo Red Room. I have been here for two years now, and I have found that no person can take tea here without quarreling. I have applied to the hotel management many times to change the color scheme but they will not. Please, please do not go away angry.

CHARLES. Do you see, Dora?

MADAME FLAMINGO. It is not you who have been quarreling, it is – it is like a great red dragon driving you to it.

DORA. But – we have said things just the same!

MADAME FLAMINGO. No, it is not you, yourselves, please. It is a red spirit in the room. Stay here, dear, and watch out for him – you will?

DORA. Yes – thank you.

MADAME FLAMINGO. Thank you.

> *(**MADAME FLAMINGO** retires.)*
>
> *(They look at each other a moment, then silently return to their cups.)*

DORA. Are you watching out for it?

CHARLES. Yes, are you?

DORA. *(Quaintly.)* Yes –

>   *(They go on drinking.)*

Finis

The Flight into Egypt

CHARACTERS

HEPZIBAH – a donkey
OUR LADY – Mary
ST. JOSEPH – her husband

SETTING

The Holy Land. Egypt.

(From time to time there are auctions of the fittings that made up the old dime museums, and at such an auction you should be able to pick up a revolving cyclorama of the Holy Land and Egypt, which is the scenery for this piece. Turn down the gaslights, for it is night in Palestine, and introduce a lady and a child on a donkey. They are accompanied by an old man on foot. The donkey's name is **HEPZIBAH.***)*

HEPZIBAH. *(For the tenth time.)* I'm tired.

OUR LADY. I know, I know.

HEPZIBAH. I'm willing to carry you as far and as fast as I can, but within reason.

ST. JOSEPH. If you didn't talk so much you'd have more strength for the journey.

HEPZIBAH. It's not my lungs that are tired, it's my legs. When I talk I don't notice how tired I am.

OUR LADY. Do as you think best, Hepzibah, but do keep moving. I can still hear Herod's soldiers behind us.

(Noise of ironmongery in the wings, right.)

HEPZIBAH. Well, I'm doing my best.

(Silence. The Tigris passes on the cyclorama.)

We must talk or I'll have to halt. We talked over the Romans and the whole political situation, and I must say again that I and every thinking person can only view such a situation with alarm, with real alarm. We talked over the village, and I don't think there's anything more to say about that. Did I remember to tell you that Issachbar's daughter's engagement had been broken?

OUR LADY. Yes.

HEPZIBAH. Well, there's always ideas. I hope I can say honestly that I am at home in ideas of all sorts. For instance, back in the yard I'm the leader of a group. Among the girls. Very interesting religious discussions, I can tell you. Very helpful.

(As some more iron is heard falling in Judaea, the Euphrates passes.)

ST. JOSEPH. Can't you hurry a bit?

HEPZIBAH. I always say to the girls: Girls, even in faith we are supposed to use our reason. No one is intended to swallow hook, line and sinker, as the saying is. Now take these children that Herod is killing. Why were they born, since they must die so soon? Can anyone answer that? Or put it another way: Why is the little boy in your arms being saved while the others must perish?

ST. JOSEPH. Is it necessary to stop?

HEPZIBAH. I was stopping for emphasis. – Mind you, it's not that I doubt. Honest discussion does not imply doubt necessarily. – What was that noise?

OUR LADY. I beg of you to make all the haste you can. The noise you hear is that of Herod's soldiers. My child will be slain while you argue about Faith. I beg of you, Hepzibah, to save him while you can.

HEPZIBAH. I assure you I'm doing the best I can, and I think I'm moving along smartly. I didn't mean that noise, anyway; it was a noise ahead. Of course, your child is dearer to you than others, but *theologically speaking*, there's no possible reason why you should escape safely into Egypt while the others should be put to the sword, as the authorized Version has it. When the Messiah comes these things will be made clear, but until then I intend to exercise my reasoning faculty. My theory is this...

OUR LADY. Hepzibah, we shall really have to beat you if you stop so often. Hepzibah, don't you remember me? Don't you remember how you fell on your knees in the stable? Don't you remember my child?

HEPZIBAH. What? What! Of course!

OUR LADY. Yes, Hepzibah.

HEPZIBAH. Let me stop just a moment and look around. No, I don't dare stop. Why didn't I recognize you before! Really, my lady, you should have spoken more sharply to me. I didn't know I could run like this; it's a pleasure. Lord, what a donkey I was to be arguing about reason while my lord was in danger.

(A pyramid flies by.)

Do you see the lights of the town yet? That's the Sphinx at the right, madam, yes, 3655 B.C. well, well, it's a queer world where the survival of the lord is dependent upon donkeys, but so it is. Why didn't you tell me before, my lady?

ST. JOSEPH. We thought you could carry us forward on your own merit.

HEPZIBAH. Oh, forgive me, madam; forgive me, sir. You don't hear any more soldiers now, I warrant you. Please don't direct me so far – excuse me – to the right, madam. That's the Nile, and there are crocodiles. My lady, may I ask one question now that we're safe?

OUR LADY. Yes, Hepzibah.

HEPZIBAH. It's this matter of faith and reason, madam. I'd love to carry back to our group of girls whatever you might say about it...

OUR LADY. Dear Hepzibah, perhaps someday. For the present just do as I do and bear your master on.

> *(More pyramids fly by; Memnon sings; the Nile moves dreamily past, and the inn is reached.)*

End of Play

Hast Thou Considered My Servant Job?

CHARACTERS

SATAN
CHRIST
JUDAS

SETTING

Another place

(Now it came to pass on the day when the sons of God came to present themselves before **SATAN** *that* **CHRIST** *also came among them. And.)*

SATAN. *(Said unto* **CHRIST.***) Whence comest thou?*

CHRIST. *(Answered* **SATAN** *and said.) From going to and fro in the earth, and from walking up and down in it.*

(And.)

SATAN. *(Said unto* **CHRIST.***) Hast thou considered my servant Judas? For there is none like him in the earth, an evil and a faithless man, one that feareth me and turneth away from God.*

(Then.)

CHRIST. *(Answered* **SATAN** *and said.) Doth Judas fear thee for naught? Hast thou not made a hedge about him, and about his house, and about all that he hath on every side? But draw back thy hand now and he will renounce thee to thy face.*

(And.)

SATAN. *(Said unto* **CHRIST.***) Behold, all that he hath is in thy power.*

(So **CHRIST** *went forth from the presence of* **SATAN.***)*

(He descended to the earth. Thirty-three years are but a moment before Satan and before God, and at the end of this moment **CHRIST** *ascends again to his own place. He passes*

on this journey before the presence of the adversary.)

SATAN. You are alone! Where is my son Judas whom I gave into your hands?

CHRIST. He follows me.

SATAN. I know what you have done. And the earth rejected you? The earth rejected you! All hell murmurs in astonishment. But where is Judas, my son and my joy?

CHRIST. Even now he is coming.

SATAN. Even Heaven, when I reigned there, was not so tedious as this waiting. Know, Prince, that I am too proud to show all my astonishment at your defeat. But now that you are swallowing your last humiliation, now that your failure has shut the mouths of the angels, I may confess that for a while I feared you. There is a fretfulness in the hearts of men. Many are inconstant, even to me. Alas, every man is not a Judas. I knew even from the beginning that you would be able, for a season, to win their hearts with your mild eloquence. I feared that you would turn to your own uses this fretfulness that visits them. But my fears were useless. Even Judas, even when my power was withdrawn from him, even Judas betrayed you. Am I not right in this?

CHRIST. You are.

SATAN. You admitted him into your chosen company. Is it permitted to me to ask for how much he betrayed you?

CHRIST. For thirty pieces of silver.

SATAN. *(After a pause.)* Am I permitted to ask to what role he was assigned in your company?

CHRIST. He held its money bags.

SATAN. *(Dazed.)* Does Heaven understand human nature as little as that? Surely the greater part of your closest companions stayed beside you to the end?

CHRIST. One stayed beside me.

SATAN. I have overestimated my enemy. Learn again, Prince, that if I were permitted to return to the earth in my own person, not for thirty years, but for thirty hours, I would seal all men to me and all the temptations in Heaven's gift could not persuade one to betray me. For I build not on intermittent dreams and timid aspirations, but on the unshakable passions of greed and lust and self-love. At last this is made clear: Judas, Judas, all the triumphs of Hell await you. Already above the eternal pavements of black marble the banquet is laid. Listen, how my nations are stirring in new hope and in new joy. Such music has not been lifted above my lakes and my mountains since the day I placed the apple of knowledge between the teeth of Adam.

> *(Suddenly the thirty pieces of silver are cast upward from the revolted hand of* **JUDAS**. *They hurtle through the skies, flinging their enormous shadows across the stars, and continue falling forever through the vast funnel of space.)*

> *(Presently* **JUDAS** *rises, the black stains about his throat and the rope of suicide.)*

What have they done to you, my beloved son? What last poor revenge have they attempted upon you? Come to me. Here there is comfort. Here all this violence can be repaired. The futile spite of Heaven cannot reach you here. But why do you not speak to me? My son, my treasure!

> *(***JUDAS** *remains with lowered eyes.)*

CHRIST. Speak to him then, my beloved son.

JUDAS. *(Still with lowered eyes, softly, to* **SATAN**.*)* Accursed be thou, from eternity to eternity.

(These two mount upward to their due place, and **SATAN** *remains to this day, uncomprehending, upon the pavement of hell.)*

End of Play

Leviathan

CHARACTERS

BRIGOMEÏDÉ – a mermaid
THE PRINCE – a shipwrecked young man
LEVIATHAN – a sea serpent

SETTING

The mid-Mediterranean

(Sunrise after a night of storm, with the sea swaying prodigiously. A great Venetian argosy has been wrecked overnight; ships and men have disappeared, leaving only the cargo spread out upon the waters. Momently new treasures from the ships' holds float upward and, reaching the surface, are swept hither and thither for miles – Persian rugs; great lengths of brocade; boxes of spice, made from tropical leaves and bound with dried vine; and an apparently interminable swathe of gray silk unwinding from its ivory standard.)

(In the foreground, a mermaid is feeling her way among the stuffs with considerable distaste. To one used to the shadowed harmonies of deep-sea color, these crimsons and oranges have no attraction. **BRIGOMEÏDÉ** *has the green, wiry hair of her kind, entangled with the friendly snail, the iridescent shoulders of all sea-women, and the gray, thin mouth.)*

(Suddenly she comes upon **THE PRINCE**. *The royal divan has been swept from the decks, and while the huge pillows are gradually soaking up the water and floating away, their* **PRINCE** *lies on them, unconscious. For a moment, the mermaid watches him open-mouthed. She steals nearer and, holding on to the tassels of seed-pearls, leans cautiously over and scans his face long and wonderingly. She sighs faintly, splashes a little in discontent, and then gazes upon him again with a frown of concentration.)*

BRIGOMEÏDÉ. It's breathing. He has not lost – what they call – the soul. I wonder where he keeps it. It is the great difference between us; we sea-people have no soul. I wonder where he keeps it! I have heard that it can be seen at times, in the eyes. Perhaps if I borrowed it from him while he slept he would never miss it. No – I will ask him for it.

(She claps her hands suddenly to awaken him, falling back, at the same time, into the water. The young man does not stir. She grows angry. She strikes the water sharply with the palms of her hands. By quick degrees a circling wind rises; great, fantastic waves rear themselves, robed in silk; they break over the divan, and **THE PRINCE** *stirs. Immediately* **BRIGOMEÏDÉ** *strokes the water to a stillness and fixes her attention on the young man.)*

THE PRINCE. My father, take not your hand away. My brothers, why have you ceased talking? Where am I? – All is lost! *Ave Maris Stella!*

BRIGOMEÏDÉ. *(Watching him intently.)* How could you sleep so – during the storm?

THE PRINCE. You – you are out of a dream. You are out of my fever. Yes, yes – the storm – you – all this is but the painting of my fever. I shall awake in Venice with the lute player fallen asleep by the window. I will call to him now and he will wake me up: Amedeo! – Lute player! Shake me out of this dream!

(The silence that follows is filled with the crackling noise as the pith fillings of the heavier cushions become saturated.)

BRIGOMEÏDÉ. *(Harshly.)* Who is it you are calling to? There is no one here, but you and me only.

THE PRINCE. Amedeo! – He does not answer: this is real. But you, you are dream; you are illusion. *Ave Maris Stella!*

BRIGOMEÏDÉ. *(Indignantly.)* I am not dream. I am not illusion. I am royal among all sea-women. – I am of the Third Order: On the three great tide days I am permitted to bind my hair with Thetis-Agrandis and wear in my ears the higher Muria.

THE PRINCE. You are out of an old ballad, taught me as a boy, and you have come back to me in the last hour on the tide of fever. In a moment my dream will have passed on from you.

BRIGOMEÏDÉ. *(Vehemently.)* You think I am only dream because…you have heard it said…we sea-folk have no souls.

THE PRINCE. Soul nor body.

BRIGOMEÏDÉ. *(More softly.)* Tell me where it is you keep your soul. Have you it always with you?

THE PRINCE. *(As a great pillow floats away from under his hand.) Flos undarum!* Save me! Deliver me! Hear my prayer!

BRIGOMEÏDÉ. Who are you speaking to? Did I not tell you there was no one here but you and me only?

THE PRINCE. You! Tell me where is shore. You can swim for days. Draw me to some island. I will give you great riches…all you desire.

BRIGOMEÏDÉ. Give me your soul. All my days I have longed for two things, black hair and a soul. I have not lacked anything else. I will draw you to your home if you will give me your soul.

THE PRINCE. *(Violently.)* It cannot be given away. No one has seen it; it cannot be felt with the hands; seen or tasted.

BRIGOMEÏDÉ. And yet they say it is the greatest thing in the world; that without it life is a cold procession of hours; that it gives all sight to the eyes, and all hearing to the ears...you are mocking me! I see in your face that you have it now!

THE PRINCE. Yes, and am about to lose it.

BRIGOMEÏDÉ. Give it to me, and I will bring up from the bottom of the sea your father and your brothers. I will return to you all the pearls that have fallen here, and draw you softly into the narrows of Venice.

THE PRINCE. *(As the water closes over him.)* Amedeo! – Lute player!

> (**BRIGOMEÏDÉ** *turns away contemptuously.*)

BRIGOMEÏDÉ. It is something you cannot touch or see. What could I do with it so?

> (**THE PRINCE** *rises, dead, entangled in scarves.* **BRIGOMEÏDÉ** *stares into his face long and earnestly.*)

It is true! There is something gone...that lay about his eyes, that troubled his mouth. The soul, perhaps.

> *(She claps her hands. From a great distance, a sea serpent swims hugely toward her. He is caught in the trailing lengths of gray brocade.)*

Gog-etar! There is no longer anything precious in this man. You may divide him among your young.

LEVIATHAN. It is terrible here, lady. These spices have made the streams unendurable. By tomorrow morning the waters will be tainted as far as Africa. Already my young are ill, lady. They lie motionless in the mud, dear lady. It is terrible to see them so...

BRIGOMEÏDÉ. I do not want to hear your troubles. Take this man away.

LEVIATHAN. Thanks, gracious lady. Perhaps these hateful essences will have made him endurable...

BRIGOMEÏDÉ. Cease!

> *(He drags* **THE PRINCE** *away. The frustrated* **BRIGOMEÏDÉ** *starts to comb the shell out of her hair, singing. Suddenly, she breaks her song and adds musingly:)*

Perhaps it is better, although your body has passed to Leviathan, still to have another part of you somewhere about the world.

End of Play

The Marriage We Deplore

CHARACTERS

EVA – an aristocrat, fifty
CHARLES – her second husband
JULIA – Eva's daughter, twenty-five
GEORGE – Eva's son, Julia's brother
PHYLLIS – George's wife

SETTING

Living room of Mrs. Eva Hibbert-Havens, Boston

(At the rise of the curtain, **EVA HIBBERT-HAVENS** *is seated, dressed for dinner, in a beautiful chair from which she does not rise until the close of the play. She is a stout, aristocratic lady, assertive but illogical. In short, a Boston grande dame. She calls to her second husband, who passes in the hall.)*

EVA. Charles! Come in, please.

CHARLES. *(Offstage, reluctantly.)* I could wait in the den, dear, until they come.

EVA. *(Firmly.)* Well, please sit down just for a minute.

*(***CHARLES HAVENS*** *comes in. He is an absentminded, slightly apologetic man in a tuxedo.)*

I haven't told Daughter yet just who the guests are. I told her to dress for dinner quietly and she'd find out later who they were.

CHARLES. *(Indifferently.)* Surely it wouldn't hurt her to say that her brother is coming to dinner.

EVA. *(Severely.)* Her brother, and her brother's wife.

CHARLES. *(Mildly.)* Yes, her brother's wife. Her sister, so to speak.

EVA. Well, if I had told Daughter that! – And I want her to look especially well tonight. *(Forcefully.)* To contrast with the rouge and tinsel of her "sister."

CHARLES. *(In surprised protest.)* But George's wife won't wear rouge and tinsel.

EVA. How do we know what George's wife won't wear? Where did he find her, I'd like to know? In a station lunchroom, very likely. In a prize shooting gallery.

CHARLES. *(Amusedly.)* In a circus, perhaps.

EVA. *(With indignation.)* I mean that my son, George Hibbert *Junior*, of the Boston Hibberts, married miles beneath him.

CHARLES. *(Absentmindedly.)* Was that her name?

EVA. As you say, he may have married a trapeze artiste.

CHARLES. *(Prosaically.)* My dear, you're always reminding me that you married beneath you when you married me. Why blame George for doing what you have found fairly satisfactory?

EVA. I blame George because he is a young man with still some prestige to make. When I married you I had been for eight years the widow of the most distinguished citizen of Boston. I could have married someone much lower than my husband's assistant manager, and still faced the world.

CHARLES. *(Gently.)* My dear, I was not your husband's assistant manager. I was his foreman.

EVA. Foreman, never. I used to see you sign his checks for him. I married my husband's sub-manager; George has married his landlady's furnace-shaker.

CHARLES. *(Shaking his head.)* He has dragged the name of Hibbert in the coal bin.

> *(Enter Daughter in evening dress. A beautiful girl of twenty-five is* **JULIA HIBBERT-HAVENS**. *She is strong-minded and so has naturally found with such a mother that concealment is the best policy. We know her to be excitingly tricky, so we are able to appreciate that her demureness in the presence of her mother is a trifle exaggerated.)*

JULIA. Well, Mother, who are these secret guests we're having tonight?

EVA. Who, indeed!

CHARLES. It's your brother George.

JULIA. And his bride?

EVA. Yes, his acquirement. He holds an indignation meeting against me for two years because I married your present father, and then he marries a Nobody and breaks the silence by inviting himself to dinner.

JULIA. Who was she?

EVA. No one seems to know; a boardinghouse girl; someone says, a waitress in a station lunchroom –

CHARLES. – You said so yourself.

EVA. Perhaps the proprietress of a shooting gallery –

CHARLES. – That was your guess.

EVA. Don't interrupt! And Charles heard that she was from a circus.

CHARLES. I didn't hear, I guessed.

EVA. Well, take your choice. Those are the rumors. George has married beneath him. It's a wonder the church allows it. Every debutante marries her chauffeur; her brother marries her lady's maid. It is a national danger. If everybody married beneath them where should we be, I'd like to know. It is the peril that lurks for democratic nations. It shows a nationwide admiration for the lower classes that is deplorable. That's what George said in his terrible letter after I had married a second time. Such names he called me! It was like Forbes-Robertson talking to his mother in *Hamlet*.*

---

* Sir Johnston Forbes-Robertson was a British actor whose daughter and son-in-law, Dinah and Vincent Sheehan, were Wilder's close friends.

CHARLES. *(Vaguely.)* Ah...is there a situation like that in *Hamlet*?

(He wanders to the bookcase.)

EVA. *(With alarm.)* No, there is not...not the slightest.

JULIA. What does it matter?

EVA. *(Anxiously.)* Do let us be frank with one another. You don't realize how difficult this is for me. What are you doing, Charles? You're not listening to me.

CHARLES. Oh, yes I was. I was seeing if I could find *Hamlet*.

EVA. Julia, I want you to burn every copy of *Hamlet* there is in the house.

JULIA. It'll spoil the sets, Mother.

EVA. There are more important things than preserving sets.

JULIA. Not in Boston.

EVA. What was I saying, Charles?

CHARLES. You wanted us to be frank with one another. My dear, I've been frank. I understand perfectly that your son was angry with you when you married me. I wrote him that I did not pretend to be more than a plain ordinary man.

JULIA. Mother, it's you that are not being frank.

EVA. *(Crying.)* Haven't I told you that she was a station restaurant waitress?

CHARLES. *(Pained.)* Dear me! What an affliction!

JULIA. All the better. Then he's in a glass house; and won't dare to throw stones at you anymore.

EVA. It's not *that* I mind. I'd like to give him a good talking to, myself. It's because I'm in a glass house.

CHARLES. *(Gently.)* My dear, seeing that this doesn't concern me, may I retire to my den until your son arrives?

(He is unnoticed.)

JULIA. Now there'll be peace in the family. No more mutual recriminations; everybody wears muzzles – in fact, they've married muzzles.

CHARLES. I daresay he's timorous about coming to see you now.

EVA. *(Sharply.)* Not at all! There's always you as a precedent.

CHARLES. *(Cowed.)* Dear me! So there is, so there is. There's the doorbell now.

EVA. Now don't anyone be tactless.

JULIA. Don't anyone mention boardinghouses or glass houses, or anything that might cause self-consciousness.

CHARLES. Am I to stay in the room all the time?

EVA. Yes; they are not to think I have any regrets. – I shall soon find out which rumor was correct.

*(Enter **GEORGE** and his wife. **GEORGE** is an obstinate young man; **PHYLLIS** is an extraordinarily pretty young girl with large blue eyes. Her hair is arranged to resemble Billie Burke's; she is exquisitely dressed and has charming manners. It is the most difficult moment in her life.)*

GEORGE. *(Kissing his mother.)* How are you, Mother? Mother, this is my wife.

EVA. *(Offering her cheek.)* You may, my dear. *(After **PHYLLIS** has kissed her.)* We meet at last, so to speak.

PHYLLIS. *(Blushing.)* Better late than never, as they say.

GEORGE. *(To **CHARLES**, shaking hands stiffly.)* How do you do, Mr. Havens. Phyllis, this is my father.

PHYLLIS. *(Faintly.)* I'm very happy to know you.

EVA. George, why don't you introduce your wife to Daughter?

JULIA. Oh, we have met, Mother.

EVA. *(In astonishment.)* When was that?

JULIA. I have called on them several times.

EVA. *(With evident displeasure.)* So *that's* how you spend your time in Atlantic City. And never say a word about it to me!

JULIA. I was saving it as a pleasant surprise.

EVA. You misjudged! – Were you ever in Boston before, Phyllis?

PHYLLIS. Unfortunately not. I have been kept pretty regularly to Atlantic City.

EVA. *(Marveling.)* And yet Boston so close!

PHYLLIS. I have occasionally run up to New York for shopping.

EVA. *(Urgently.)* Charles! My smelling salts – in the hall.

(He gets them.)

But naturally from your position in the station you were able to see the trains depart for Boston.

PHYLLIS. *(Agreeably.)* Oh, yes. There are trains.

EVA. *(Nodding her head enigmatically.)* Hmm – yes... yes. Did you find it monotonous? – Standing over the counter, long hours...?

PHYLLIS. *(At sea.)* You mean, did we come by boat?

JULIA. No, dear, Mother means: Did you find the trip longer than you expected?

PHYLLIS. *(To her.)* I like traveling.

EVA. I see! Naturally. How fortunate. There must be long waits while the tents are being nailed down. – Then there's the long, hot parade.

PHYLLIS. *(To* **GEORGE**.*)* I'm afraid – I do not understand…

GEORGE. You mean, Mother – ?

JULIA. *(To the rescue.)* By parade, Mother means the boardwalk at Atlantic City we all hear so much about.

PHYLLIS. *(To* **EVA**, *brightly.)* Oh, no. It's a pleasure, I assure you. And on the hottest days there are the awnings – that's what you meant by "tents."

EVA. Yes, yes. But no doubt there are tents, too. Fortune tellers, and –

PHYLLIS. – A very few. –

EVA. – And among them, the shooting gallery.

PHYLLIS. *(Seeking light.)* The shooting gallery?

EVA. *(Boldly.)* The one you were interested in.

(At last **PHYLLIS** *is completely perplexed.)*

PHYLLIS. *(In a pretty confusion.)* I'm afraid I'm very dull. But I've heard of the subtlety – the wit – of Boston conversation. I have always lived quietly with my mother in our little home on the North Shore. I've had little experience –

JULIA. – Don't apologize, Phyllis. Mother has a playful way you'll understand when you get to know her better.

EVA. I was not aware of it.

CHARLES. *(Soothingly.)* Now Eva! You know you're famous for your wit.

GEORGE. It has developed then in the last year – amazingly.

EVA. *(Retorting.)* Think of what I've had to bear.

GEORGE. I warned you in good time.

(Fortunately, dinner is announced at this point.)

EVA. *(Rising and repeating a formula used by all Boston hostesses at informal dinners to relatives.)* We live very simply, but of such as it is we try to obtain the best, and to that you are always welcome.

*(She leads the way out with **CHARLES**.)*

PHYLLIS. *(Turning, at the front of the stage; plaintively.)* I don't understand your mother at all, George –

*(She sees **JULIA** and runs to her.)*

When are you to be married, Julia?

JULIA. *(Smiling down at her happily.)* On Saturday afternoon at four o' the clock.

PHYLLIS. Why at four?

JULIA. Because they don't let the dear boy out of the factory until three; and he says he *must* brush his hair.

(They go on into dinner.)

End of Play

The Message
and Jehanne

CHARACTERS

CHARLES – the goldsmith
TULLIO – the apprentice
LADY JEHANNE – a beauty

SETTING

A goldsmith's shop in Renaissance Paris

(The tops of the shop windows are just above the level of the street, and through them we see the procession of shoes, any one of them a novel or a play or a poem. In the workshop one finds not only medals and salad forks for prelates, but unexpected things, a viola d'amore and folios ruled for music.)

*(**TULLIO** enters from the street and confronts his master, **CHARLES OF BENICET**. **TULLIO** stands with his back to the door and lets his breath out slowly, as one who has just accomplished a great work.)*

CHARLES. *(Rubbing his hands.)* So you delivered the rings?

TULLIO. Yes, master.

CHARLES. And what did my little brown Jacquenetta say?

TULLIO. She twice read the verse you had written in the ring. Then she looked at me. Then she looked at the ring. "It is too cold," she said.

CHARLES. Too cold?

TULLIO. She said: "But...but I suppose it's what must go inside a ring!" Then she kissed the ring and bade me tell you she loved it.

CHARLES. *(Arrested and puzzled.)* Too cold, the verse! – But I'll make her another. We forget how they love us. And the other ring? Did you deliver the Graf's ring to the Lady Jehanne herself?

TULLIO. Yes, master. Into her very own hand. Her house is very old and in a bad part of the city. As I crossed the court and stood in the hall a great German, with fierce eyebrows, came in from the street with me.

CHARLES. Yes, that's the one she's to marry.

TULLIO. He asked me loudly what I had there. And I said, a box for the Lady Jehanne, and that it was for her hand alone, and I ran to the landing on the stairs. Then she came out herself. He cried out upon her: what gift was she receiving? And was it from a certain English student at Padua? And she said: "No, Baron, it is the wedding ring you have sent me." And when I gave it to her she went in, very white, and without speaking to him. Then I went to Jacquenetta's with the other ring, and she gave me some supper.

CHARLES. Too cold, the verse! Start putting up the shutters; I must go and see her.

> *(It has been growing darker. Suddenly a pair of shoes, a poem these, descends from the crowd, and **TULLIO** opens the door to a knock. A beautiful lady gives Christian greeting, and a seat is made for her among the littered chairs. She sits in silence until **TULLIO** has lighted the candles and retired.)*

JEHANNE. You are Charles of Benicet, master in precious metals?

CHARLES. *Carolus Benizentius auro argentoque magister,* and composer of music to God and to such men whose ears He chooses to open.

JEHANNE. You are a composer too?

CHARLES. They are callings like two sisters who have ever their arms about the other's neck. When I have made a wedding ring I compose a motet thereto. The boy who calls to see if the candlesticks are done takes back with him a Mass.

JEHANNE. *(Without a breath.)* Oh!

CHARLES. Can I serve you with music or with metals?

JEHANNE. You have served me today. I am the Lady Jehanne.

CHARLES. Ah, yes! The ring was unsatisfactory? I can make another tonight. I shall set about it at once.

JEHANNE. No, master. The ring is very beautiful.

CHARLES. *(After a pause, pretending to be embarrassed.)* I am overjoyed that it pleases you.

JEHANNE. *(Suddenly.)* The verses that you put in the rings – where do you find *them*?

CHARLES. Unless there is a special request, my lady, I put in nothing but the traditional legend: *fidelitas carior vita.*

JEHANNE. *(Without reproach.)* But there are liberties you allow yourself? Master, what meant you when you wrote within my ring?

CHARLES. My lady!

JEHANNE. *(Giving him the ring.)* Graf Klaus addresses me thus.

CHARLES. *(Reading around the inside of the ring.)* "As the hermit his twilight, the countryman his holiday, the worshiper his peace, so do I love thee." It was the wrong ring that was delivered to you, my lady.

JEHANNE. It has broken my will. I am in fight for Padua. My family are truly become nothing but sparrows and God will feed them.

End of Play

Mozart and
the Gray Steward

CHARACTERS

CONSTANZE – Mozart's wife
MOZART – the composer
THE GRAY STEWARD – a mysterious visitor

SETTING

Mozart's quarters in Vienna

(**MOZART** *is seated at a table in a mean room orchestrating* The Magic Flute. *Leaves of ruled paper are strewn about the floor. His wife enters in great excitement.*)

CONSTANZE. There's someone come to see you, someone important. Pray God, it's a commission from court.

MOZART. *(Unmoved.)* Not while Salieri's alive.

CONSTANZE. Put on your slippers, dear. It's someone dressed all in gray, with a gray mask over his eyes, and he's come in a great coach with its coat of arms all covered up with gray cloth. Pray God, it's a commission from court for a *Te Deum* or something.

(*She tidies up the room in six gestures.*)

MOZART. Not while Salieri's alive.

CONSTANZE. But, now, do be nice, 'Gangl, please. We must have some money, my treasure. Just listen to him and say "yes" and "thank you," and then you and I'll talk it over after he's gone.

(*She holds his coat.*)

Come, put this on. Step into your slippers.

MOZART. *(Sighing.)* I'm not well. I'm at home. I'm at work. There's not a single visitor in the whole world that could interest me. Bring him in.

CONSTANZE. *(Adjusting his stock.)* Now don't be proud. Just accept.

(*She hurries out and presently reenters preceding the visitor. The visitor is dressed from head to foot in gray silk. His bright eyes look out through the holes in a narrow gray silk mask. He holds to his nose a gray, perfumed handkerchief. One would say: an elegant undertaker.)*

THE GRAY STEWARD. Kappelmeister Mozart, *servus*. Gracious lady, *servus*.

MOZART. *Servus.*

THE GRAY STEWARD. Revered and noble master, wherever music reigns, wherever genius is valued, the name of Wolfgang Amadeus Mozart is...

MOZART. Sir, I have always been confused by compliments and beg you to spare me that mortification by proceeding at once to the cause of your visit...the...the honor of your visit.

THE GRAY STEWARD. Revered master, before I lay my business before you, may I receive your promise that – whether you accept my commission or not – you both will...

MOZART. I promise you our secrecy, unless our silence would prove dishonorable to me or injurious to someone else. Pray continue.

THE GRAY STEWARD. Know then, gracious and revered genius, that I come from a prince who combines all the qualities of birth, station, generosity and wisdom.

MOZART. Ha! A European secret.

THE GRAY STEWARD. His Excellency moreover has just sustained a bitter misfortune. He has lately lost his wife and consort, a lady who was the admiration of her court and the sole light of her bereaved husband's life. Therefore, His Excellency, my master, commissions you to compose a Requiem Mass in honor of this lady. He asks you to pour into it the height of your invention and that wealth of melody and harmony that have made you the glory of our era. And for this music he asks leave to pay you the sum of four hundred crowns – two hundred now, and the second two hundred crowns when you deliver the first four numbers.

MOZART. Well, Constanze, I must not be proud.

THE GRAY STEWARD. There is but one proviso.

MOZART. Yes, I heard it. The work must represent the height of my invention.

THE GRAY STEWARD. That was an easy assumption, master. The proviso is this: you shall let His Excellency have this music as an anonymous work, and you shall never by any sign, by so much as the nod of your head, acknowledge that the work is yours.

MOZART. And His Excellency is not aware that the pages I may compose at the height of my invention may be their own sufficient signature?

THE GRAY STEWARD. That may be. Naturally my master will see to it that no other composer will ever be able to claim the work as his.

MOZART. Quick, give me your paper and I will sign it. Leave your two hundred crowns with my wife at the foot of the stairs. Come back in August and you will have the first four numbers. *Servus. Servus.*

THE GRAY STEWARD. *(Backing out.) Servus,* master. *Servus*, madame.

> (**CONSTANZE** *returns in a moment and looks anxiously toward her husband.*)

CONSTANZE. A visit from Heaven, 'Gangl. Now you can go into the country. Now you can drink all the Bohemian water in the world.

MOZART. *(Bitterly.)* Good. And just at a time when I was contemplating a Requiem Mass. But for *myself*. However, I must not be proud.

CONSTANZE. *(Trying to divert him.)* Who can these people be? Try and think.

MOZART. Oh, there's no mystery about that. It's the Count Von Walsegg. He composes himself. But for the most part he buys string quartets from us; he erases the signatures and has them played in his castle. The courtiers flatter him and pretend that they have guessed him to be the composer. He does not deny it. He tries to appear confused. And now he has succeeded in composing a Requiem. But that will reduce my pride.

CONSTANZE. You know he will only be laughed at. The music will speak for itself. Heaven wanted to give us four hundred crowns –

MOZART. – And Heaven went about it humorously.

CONSTANZE. What was his wife like?

MOZART. Her impudences smelt to Heaven. She dressed like a page and called herself Cherubin. Her red cheeks and her black teeth and her sixty years are in my mind now.

CONSTANZE. *(After a pause.)* We'll give back the money. You can write the music, without writing it for them.

MOZART. No, I like this game. I like it for its very falseness. What does it matter who signs such music or to whom it is addressed?

> *(He flings himself upon the sofa and turns his face to the wall.)*

For whom do we write music? – for musicians? Salieri! For patrons? Von Walsegg! For the public? The Countess Von Walsegg! – I shall write this Requiem, but it shall be for myself, since I am dying.

CONSTANZE. My beloved, don't talk so! Go to sleep.

> *(She spreads a shawl over his body.)*

How can you say such things? Imagine even thinking such a thing! You will live many years and write countless beautiful pages. We will return the money and refuse the commission. Then the matter will be closed. Now go to sleep, my treasure.

> (*She goes out, quietly closing the door behind her.* **MOZART**, *at the mercy of his youth, his illness, and his genius, is shaken by a violent fit of weeping. The sobs gradually subside, and he falls asleep. In his dream,* **THE GRAY STEWARD** *returns.*)

THE GRAY STEWARD. Mozart! Turn and look at me. You know who I am.

MOZART. *(Not turning.)* You are the steward of the Count Von Walsegg. Go tell him to write his own music. I will not stain my pen to celebrate his lady, so let the foul bury the foul.

THE GRAY STEWARD. Lie then against the wall, and learn that it is Death itself that commissions...

MOZART. Death is not so fastidious. Death carries no perfumed handkerchief.

THE GRAY STEWARD. Lie then against the wall. Know first that all the combinations of circumstance can suffer two interpretations, the apparent and the real.

MOZART. Then speak, sycophant, I know the apparent one. What other reading can this humiliation bear?

THE GRAY STEWARD. It is Death itself that commands you this Requiem. You are to give a voice to all those millions sleeping, who have no one but you to speak for them. There lie the captains and the thieves, the queens and the drudges, while the evening of their earthly remembrance shuts in, and from that great field rises an eternal *miserere nobis*. Only through the intercession of great love, and of great art, which is love, can that despairing cry be eased. Was that not sufficient cause for this commission to be anonymous?

MOZART. *(Drops trembling on one knee beside the couch.)* Forgive me.

THE GRAY STEWARD. And it was for this that the pretext and mover was chosen from among the weakest and vainest of humans. Death has her now, and all her folly has passed into the dignity and grandeur of her state. Where is your pride now? Here are her slippers and her trinkets. Press them against your lips. Again! Again! Know henceforth that only he who has kissed the leper can enter the kingdom of art.

MOZART. I have sinned, yet grant me one thing. Grant that I may live to finish the Requiem.

THE GRAY STEWARD. No! No!

(And it remains unfinished.)

End of Play

Nascuntur Poetae

CHARACTERS
THE WOMAN IN THE CHLAMYS
THE BOY
THE WOMAN IN DEEP RED

SETTING
A painting of Piero di Cosimo

(We are gazing into some strange, incomprehensible painting of Piero di Cosimo – a world of pale blues and greens, of abrupt peaks in agate and of walled cities, of flying red stags with hounds at their throats, and of lions in tears beside their crowns. On the roads are seen traveling companies, in no haste and often lost in contemplation of the sky. A **BOY** *sits on a rock in the foreground. He is listening to the words of a* **WOMAN DRESSED IN A CHLAMYS** *that takes on the color of the objects about her.)*

THE WOMAN IN THE CHLAMYS. In a far valley, boy, sit those who in their lifetime have possessed some special gift of eye or ear or finger. There they sit apart, choosing their successors. And when on the winds toward birth the souls of those about to live are borne past them, they choose the brighter spirits that cry along that wind. And you were chosen.

THE BOY. For what gift, lady, did the choice fall? Am I to mould in clay, or paint? Shall I sing or mime, lady? What choice fell on me and from what master?

THE WOMAN IN THE CHLAMYS. It is enough to know that you were chosen.

THE BOY. What further remains to be done? You have poured on my eyes and ears and mouth the divine ointment; you have laid on my tongue the burning ember. Why do we delay?

THE WOMAN IN THE CHLAMYS. Be not so eager for life. Too soon you will be shaken by breath; too soon and too long you will be tossed in the tumult of the senses.

THE BOY. I am not afraid of life. I will astonish it. – Why are we delaying?

THE WOMAN IN THE CHLAMYS. My sister is coming now. Listen to her.

> (**THE WOMAN IN THE CHLAMYS** *withdraws and gives place to her sister, whose feet stir not the shells upon the path. She wears a robe of deep and noble red and bears in her hands a long, golden chain hung about with pendants. Her face is fixed in concentration and compassion, like the face of one taking part in a sacrifice of great moment.*)

THE BOY. All is ready. What do you come to do?

THE WOMAN IN DEEP RED. My sister has given you the gifts of pride and of joy. But those are not all.

THE BOY. What gifts remain? I have been chosen. I am ready.

THE WOMAN IN DEEP RED. Those gifts are vain without these. He who carries much gold stumbles. I bring the dark and necessary gifts. This golden chain...

THE BOY. *(With mounting fear.)* Your face is shadowed. Draw back; take back all the gifts, if I must accept these also.

THE WOMAN IN DEEP RED. Too late. Too late. You had no choice in this. You must bow your head.

THE BOY. I am trembling. My knees are hot with my tears.

THE WOMAN IN DEEP RED. Since only tears can give sight to the eyes.

(She drops the chain about his neck.)

THE BOY. Then am I permitted to know the meaning of these pendants?

THE WOMAN IN DEEP RED. This is a tongue of fire. It feeds upon the brain. It is a madness that in a better country has a better name.

THE BOY. These are mysteries. Give them no names.

THE WOMAN IN DEEP RED. This is a leaf of laurel from a tree not often plucked. You shall know pride and the shining of the eyes – of that I do not speak now.

THE BOY. And this, lady?

THE WOMAN IN DEEP RED. That is a staff and signifies the journey that awaits you your life long; for you are homeless.

THE BOY. And this…this is of crystal…

THE WOMAN IN DEEP RED. That is yours alone, and you shall smart for it. It is wonderful and terrible. Others shall know a certain peace, and shall live well enough in the limits of the life they know; but you shall be forever hindered. For you there shall be ever beyond the present a lost meaning and a more meaningful love.

THE BOY. Take back the chain. Take back your gifts. Take back life. For at its end what can there be that is worth such pain?

THE WOMAN IN DEEP RED. *(Slowly drawing back into the shadow of the wood.)* Farewell, child of the muses, playfellow in the bird-haunted groves. The life of man awaits you, the light laughter and the misery in the same day, in the selfsame hour the trivial and the divine. You are to give it a voice. Among the bewildered and the stammering thousands you are to give it a voice and to mark its meaning. Farewell, child of the muses, playfellow in the bird-haunted…

*(***THE WOMAN IN THE CHLAMYS** *returns.)*

THE WOMAN IN THE CHLAMYS. You must go now. Listen to that wind. It is the great fan of time that whirls on the soul for a season.

THE BOY. Stay a moment. I am not yet brave.

> *(She leads him into a grotto and the young soul and his chain are lost in the profound shade.)*

End of Play

Now the Servant's Name Was Malchus

CHARACTERS

THE ANGEL GABRIEL – secretary and soldier
OUR LORD
MALCHUS – of the Bible

SETTING

The house of the lord

(In his Father's house are many mansions, and it is from the windows of one of them that he stands looking out upon the clockwork of the skies. With the precision that is possible only to things dead in themselves, the stars weave incessantly their interlocking measures. At intervals the blackest pockets of space give birth to a nebula, whirling in new anguish, but for the most part the sky offers only its vast stars, eased in the first gradations of their cooling, and fulfilling happily and with a faint humming sound the long loops of their appointment.)

(To him comes **GABRIEL**.*)*

GABRIEL. There are some unusually urgent petitions here... There's this colonel on a raft in the Bengal Sea. – Here again is the widow and her two daughters in Moscow. A lady in Rome.

(He lays some papers on the table.)

Besides, there is someone outside who wishes to speak to you. He says he knew you on earth. I think he has something to complain of, even here.

OUR LORD. Let him wait a moment.

(There is loud rapping at the door.)

GABRIEL. There he is again.

OUR LORD. Then let him in.

*(***GABRIEL*** admits* **MALCHUS** *and goes out.)*

MALCHUS. Please, sir, excuse me being so hasty, but I had to speak to you about something.

OUR LORD. You are displeased with Heaven?

MALCHUS. Oh no, sir – except for one thing.

OUR LORD. We will talk about it in a minute. Come by the window and look. Can you tell me which of those stars is mine?

MALCHUS. Lord, all are yours, surely.

OUR LORD. No, only one is mine, for only one bears living things upon it. And where there is no life I have no power. All the stars save one are lifeless; not even a blade of grass pushes through their powder or their fame. But one of them is so crowded with event that Heaven itself is scarcely able to attend to its needs. – But you are not interested?

MALCHUS. Oh, sir, it was so long ago that I was there that I cannot be expected to... Even my children's children have long since left it. I cannot be very interested. Since I am so happy here – except for one thing. But I should like to see it again. Which is it, sir?

OUR LORD. There, see! See where it floats for a moment out of a green mist. If your ears were accustomed to it as mine are, you would hear what I hear: the sigh as it turns. Now, what is it you want of me?

MALCHUS. Well, as you know, I was the High Priest's servant in the garden when you were taken. Sir, it's hardly worth mentioning.

OUR LORD. No, no. Speak out.

MALCHUS. And one of your fellows took out his sword and cut off my ear.

OUR LORD. Yes.

MALCHUS. It's...it's hardly worth mentioning. Most of the time, Lord, we're very happy up here and nothing disturbs us at our games. But whenever someone on earth thinks about us we are aware of it, pleasantly or unpleasantly. A sort of something crosses our mind. And because I'm in your book someone is always reading about me and thinking about me for a moment, and in the middle of my games I feel it. Especially at this season, when your death is celebrated, no moment goes by without this happening. And what they think is, that I'm ridiculous.

OUR LORD. I see. And you want your name to be erased from the book?

MALCHUS. *(Eagerly.)* Yes, sir. I thought you could just make the pages become blank at that place.

OUR LORD. Now that you have come here everything that you wish is granted to you. You know that.

MALCHUS. Yes, sir; thank you, sir.

OUR LORD. But stay a minute. At this season, Malchus, a number of people are thinking of me, too.

MALCHUS. Yes, Lord, but as good, as great...

OUR LORD. But, Malchus, I am ridiculous too.

MALCHUS. Oh, no, no!

OUR LORD. Ridiculous because I suffered from the delusion that after my death I could be useful to men.

MALCHUS. They don't say that!

OUR LORD. And that my mind lay under a malady that many a doctor could cure. And that I have deceived and cheated millions and millions of souls who in their extremity called on me for the aid I had promised. They did not know that I died like any other man and their prayers mounted into vain air, for I no longer exist. My promises were so vast that I am either divine or ridiculous.

(Pause.)

OUR LORD. Malchus, will you stay and be ridiculous with me?

MALCHUS. Yes, sir, I'll stay. I'm glad to stay. Though in a way I haven't any right to be there. I wasn't even the High Priest's servant; I only held his horse every now and then. And…and I used to steal a little – only you've forgiven me that. Sure, I'm glad to stay.

OUR LORD. Thank you, Malchus.

MALCHUS. *(Smiling.)* It isn't even true in the book. It was my left ear and not my right.

OUR LORD. Yes, the book isn't always true about me, either.

MALCHUS. Excuse my troubling you, sir. Good day.

OUR LORD. Good day, Malchus.

> (**MALCHUS** *goes out.* **GABRIEL** *enters discreetly and lays down some more papers.*)

GABRIEL. *(In a low voice.)* The raft has capsized, sir, on the Bengal Sea, and the colonel will be here at once. The women in Moscow…

End of Play

The Penny That Beauty Spent

CHARACTERS

CLAIRE-LOUISE "LA GRACILE" – a dancer
QUINTE – her husband
THE JEWELER

SETTING

A jeweler's shop in Paris

(The little heartbreak takes place in a rococo jeweler's shop. The shop is elegantly small and elegantly polished. The few jewels and the few pieces of brocade are tossed from surface to surface in a world of glass, from the chandelier to the mirrors and from the mirrors to the cases. It is royalty's own place of purchase, and the great egotistical head is present in bust and in miniature and on the backs of spoons. The old jeweler, enigmatic and smiling, is suddenly called to the door by a great clatter. A girl enters, borne on the shoulders of a boy little older than herself. **LA GRACILE** *is thin and pinch-faced, but long penury has only made her the more elfin. Illness is already writing its progress in the eyes and on the brow of* **QUINTE**. *But they are deliciously happy and full of their secrets.* **QUINTE** *lifts her onto the counter and draws back.)*

LA GRACILE. While you are with me I need never touch the ground. You can carry me from cushion to cushion.

QUINTE. And on your gravestone will be inscribed: "Here lies an exquisite dancer, she who never touched the ground."

LA GRACILE. And beside mine yours will read: "Here lies her husband, the soul of her life, the sole of her shoes."

THE JEWELER. Mademoiselle is in pain? The feet of mademoiselle are in pain?

(After she has recovered, with **QUINTE**, *from the whirlwind of intimate amusement that this preposterous idea has caused them:)*

LA GRACILE. No. I am the new dancer. I am La Gracile. Except when I dance I wear nothing on my feet but little velvet pockets. So when I am not wearing my practice slippers, my husband carries me about.

THE JEWELER. Oh, you are La Gracile. We have already heard of your great success last night. The king is delighted with you.

LA GRACILE. *(Shrilly, clapping her hands.)* Yes, yes, yes. I was a great success. Even the king's favorite, Madame d'Hautillon, was jealous. She tried to stand on my foot. They call me the moth of Versailles.

THE JEWELER. And now the king has sent you here to choose a present for yourself.

LA GRACILE. How did you know?

THE JEWELER. The king sends to me for a gift every young lady who pleases him. Madame d'Hautillon was here last.

LA GRACILE. *(Chattering on.)* I want nothing myself. It is to be for Quinte. A chronometer, please, that strikes every hour with a gavotte and midnight with a saraband.

QUINTE. Nothing for me, Claire-Louise. When my cough returns it will shake every ornament off me, the buttons from my coat, the rings from my thin fingers. You must have something in pearls.

LA GRACILE. Silly Quinte, I want nothing.

QUINTE. But I suppose... You must wear something for the king.

LA GRACILE. *(Suddenly under a passing cloud of melancholy, resting her cheek on his hair, plaintively.)* I do not want a great showy pin on my breast. I want only a little white daisy from our beloved Brittany, from Grandmother's field that had too many stones.

QUINTE. Tell her what you have, Monsieur Jeweler.

THE JEWELER. Mademoiselle will look at this chain? Its art is secret. It is painted gold, the work of aged nuns in Hamburg.

QUINTE. Oh look, Claire-Louise, this flower for your hair. Many topazes were splintered to powder on the wheel before this perfect one.

THE JEWELER. Etiquette forbids, mademoiselle, your buying that; it happens to be the very thing that Madame d'Hautillon bought for herself.

LA GRACILE. *(Arousing herself, imperiously.)* Have you a little fat chronometer with many jewels in it?

THE JEWELER. *(Proffering a tray.)* The best in Paris.

LA GRACILE. *(Giving one to* **QUINTE.***)* That is for you, Quinte, from myself and from the dull king. Like my thoughts, it will rest on your heart, but long after it is sold as wire and rust my love will go on in the land where clocks do not mark off one sad moment from another.

QUINTE. *(With tears.)* Claire-Louise, it can be of no pleasure to me. In a while it will only please me because it is a little cool in my hot hand.

LA GRACILE. *(Softly, in pain.)* Courage, dearest Quinte, courage.

THE JEWELER. *(Interrupting formally.)* Remember, mademoiselle, that etiquette demands that you will choose a present that His Majesty will admire on you.

LA GRACILE. *(Stormily.)* I shall choose what I please.

THE JEWELER. *(Insinuatingly.)* Your life is only to please the king. He has chosen you. By sending you here he is telling you that.

LA GRACILE. You are mistaken... But I am only a poor thin dancer that...that has worked too hard. Besides, this is my husband.

THE JEWELER. *(Smiling.)* No, mademoiselle, he is not your husband.

> (**LA GRACILE** *jumps down and walks away, weeping bitterly, her little feet-sacks flopping against the polished floor. She suddenly turns with blazing eyes.*)

LA GRACILE. I shall run away to Brittany... I shall scratch his eyes out.

> (**THE JEWELER** *smiles at this foolish notion and leans across the counter, holding toward her a great jewel-encrusted buckle.*)

(Wildly.) Even though all Versailles kill me with steel pins, Quinte shall have the watch.

> *(But he has fallen among the gilt chairs.)*

End of Play

Proserpina and the Devil:
A Play for Marionettes

CHARACTERS

THE MANAGER
THE FIRST MANIPULATOR
THE SECOND MANIPULATOR

The Puppets:
PROSERPINA, DEMETER, HERMES, and **DEVIL**

SETTING

A puppet show, Venice, 1640 A.D.

THE MANAGER. *(Winningly.)* Citizens and little citizens! We are going to give you a delicious foretaste of our great performance this afternoon, to which the whole world is coming. This is a pantomime about how a beautiful girl named Proserpina was snatched away by the Devil, and how her mother searched for her over all the hills of the world, and how at last she was able to bring her back to the earth for six months out of every year.

THE FIRST MANIPULATOR. *(Behind the scenes.)* Let go them strings.

THE MANAGER. At our great performance this afternoon this same play will be given *with words;* and besides it the story of the brave Melusina and her wanderings when she was driven out of Parma.

THE SECOND MANIPULATOR. *(His voice rising in anger.)* You don't have to show me!

THE MANAGER. On with the play! – But don't forget to bring your rich aunts this afternoon. *(To the* **MANIPULATORS.***)* Hurry through with it. I'm off for a cup of wine.

> *(The curtain rises with indecent haste and shows the underworld. The rivers Styx and Acheron have been replaced by a circular piece of cloth, sulphur-colored, with waves delicately embroidered about the margin. This is the Lake of Wrath, and in it are seen floating arms and legs – all that are left, alas, of great puppets, Abraham, Penelope and Jephtha's daughter, Midas, and Harlequin. Beside the lake,* **PROSERPINA** *is straying, robed in bluish black as one anticipating*

> *grief. Pluto – now a medieval **SATAN** – is stealthily approaching her. Suddenly, **PROSERPINA** throws up her arms, runs to him, and buries her face in his scarlet bosom. Noah's Ark – mutely protesting against the part it must play, with all its Christianized animals within it, of Charon's barge – is lowered from the proscenium, and the curtain falls.)*

THE FIRST MANIPULATOR. *(Sotto voce.)* Beard of Medusa! You made her run in the wrong direction: The hussy courted death. Didn't I tell you he was to chase her three times around the lake?

THE SECOND MANIPULATOR. *(Sulkily.)* I don't care. A person can't tell which is his right hand and which is his left in this place.

THE FIRST MANIPULATOR. Here, you let me take her; you take the Devil. – Got the orange?

> *(When the puppets are next seen, **PROSERPINA** is exhibiting grief in pantomime. Her lord with affectionate gestures urges her to eat of a yellow pomegranate. Sadly she puts it to her mouth. With an odd recollection of the Garden of Eden, she tempts him into eating the remaining half. They go out cheerlessly.)*

All right for that. Now I'll take the mother and the Devil. You take the other fellow and the daughter.

> *(**DEMETER**, a handsome Italian matron in a wide gown of brocade, enters with her arms outstretched. At her elbow, **HERMES**, the Archangel Gabriel, guides her through the Lake of Perdition. **PROSERPINA** and her husband return and throw up their hands in amazement. Again, the frantic girl runs in the wrong direction and casts herself into the*

arms of **SATAN**. **DEMETER** *tries to draw her away, but a matter of pins and hooks-and-eyes prevents her rescue.)*

Oh, you Gazoon! You lack-eyed Silenus! Your hands are nothing but feet.

THE SECOND MANIPULATOR. The Devil take your show and you with it.

(The altercation behind the scenes grows out of bounds, and one blow knocks down the stage. The **ARCHANGEL** *falls upon the pavement and is cherished by gamins unto the third generation; the* **DEVIL** *rolls into the lake;* **PROSERPINA** *is struck by a falling cloud, and lies motionless on her face;* **DEMETER** *by reason of the stiffness of her brocade stands upright, viewing with staring eyes the ills of her daughter.)*

End of Play

The Song of
Maria Bentedos

CHARACTERS

GERALD MARVIN
MRS. MARVIN
MARIA BENTEDOS

*(The rising young composer, **GERALD MARVIN**, is tearing up and down his room in an awful state, hands plunging into his coat pockets, feet kicking rugs and music stands from his way, mouth blowing impotently, and at intervals bellowing an unrecognizable melody.)*

*(The door opens to firm, competent, young **MRS. MARVIN**, in hat and veil, just come in.)*

MRS. MARVIN. What's the matter, dear?

GERALD. Sit down; listen and tell me what this melody is.

(He roars it out.)

MRS. MARVIN. I can't tell a thing that way. You must play it on the piano.

GERALD. Well, if you knew it at all, you'd know it that way.

(Plays it in simple chords.)

MRS. MARVIN. I don't think I ever heard it. Why are you so upset about it? It doesn't seem very wonderful.

GERALD. It's been going through my head all day, and I don't know whether I made it up, or whether I heard it somewhere else. I want to work it into the finale of my Sonata, if it's my own, but if it isn't, I just have to give it up.

MRS. MARVIN. Just use it anyway, dear. If you do it nicely, they'll forgive you.

GERALD. What, have myself known as unable to write a melody? And have you go to *Verdi* for the finales of my Sonatas! Nelly, you're a –

MRS. MARVIN. *(Peremptorily.)* Control yourself! I've known your penny tempers too long. You've made a baby of yourself all over the world, from Lisbon – you remember your signet ring at Lisbon – to Vladivostock, where you thought you could speak Russian. Now I want you to give up all that, now we've settled down. It doesn't do any good to call me a fool. Give me the paper with this tune written on it; I'll sing it to Herr Karmin over the telephone and see if he knows it. If you lose control again, I will not take the trouble to get up any more little bohemian suppers for your friends. They're too hard work to do without gratitude.

> *(She takes the paper from the piano rack and goes out.)*

> *(**GERALD**, somewhat chastened, goes back to the piano, plays the melody over again and slowly works himself into desperation again. He fixes a gloomy eye on the leg of the piano and murmurs: "I'll go mad!" Then he gets up behind a music stand and directs a huge crowd and orchestra of thousands, through several variations, singing heartily himself. The hall door, which was left ajar, is slowly opened, and a young woman of olive complexion and black eyes stands there with a basket of lace, etc.)*

GERALD. What do *you* want?

MARIA. Signor want some lace?

GERALD. No. Why should I want some lace? I thought they didn't allow peddlers in these apartments.

MARIA. *(She slips in.)* Look, Signor, at the beautiful lace. One can give it to the Signorita. It is like the white in water of soap; It is like little fogs in the sky.

GERALD. *(Roaring.)* Go – *(Looking toward the door; softer.)* Go away.

MARIA. No sewing? Nothing?

GERALD. No.

MARIA. No torn clothes?

GERALD. *(Hurling off his coat and tearing off a button.)* No, nothing.

MARIA. *(Excitedly.)* Signor has torn a button off his coat.

GERALD. *(Ruefully.)* The devil!

MARIA. Give me.

GERALD. There!

> *(Throws them to her. She sets to work immediately. Then **GERALD** takes his music stand and starts directing her through the first measures of the evasive melody. Then he breaks off, goes to the door and calls:)*

Call Kennedy and Graham, too. *(Listening to his wife on the phone.)* No F sharp there; how do you expect them to recognize it when you don't pay any attention to the key signature?

> *(**MRS. MARVIN** appears at the door. **GERALD** helps the piano to hide **MARIA**.)*

MRS. MARVIN. *(From the door.)* Control yourself. I will not call up another person until you sit down quietly and read your new German magazine.

GERALD. All right, I will.

MRS. MARVIN. Herr Karmin says he never heard it, and it doesn't sound like one of the three B's.

GERALD. Thanks awfully, Nelly –

MRS. MARVIN. There's your magazine.

> *(She goes. He sits down quietly at his folio, and almost forgets the industrious **MARIA**,*

who starts to sing the melody to herself. At the end of it, **GERALD** *jumps up.)*

GERALD. *(Excitedly.)* What's that you're singing?

MARIA. Song my mother sing me.

GERALD. Where?

MARIA. *(Holding up coat.)* Finish! Look!

GERALD. Where did you learn that song?

MARIA. Barcelona.

GERALD. Of Course. Look here, come and sing it to me tomorrow. Hurry away now. Catch!

(He throws a dollar.)

MARIA. *(Transported.)* Gracias, Signor

GERALD. *(Equally delighted.)* Gracias yourself.

(**MARIA** *permits herself to be hustled out.)*

(Goes to the other door and calls.) All right, Nelly, I know what it is. One of those folk songs we heard in Spain. Thanks for your trouble...

(And that's all.)

End of Play

www.ingramcontent.com/pod-product-compliance
Lightning Source LLC
Chambersburg PA
CBHW072007290426
44109CB00018B/2166